Brian Davies is a Dominican Friar and
Lecturer in Philosophy at Blackfriars,
Oxford.

An OPUS book

An Introduction to the Philosophy of Religion

OPUS General Editors

Keith Thomas
Alan Ryan
Peter Medawar

Brian Davies

An Introduction to the Philosophy of Religion

Oxford New York Toronto Melbourne

OXFORD UNIVERSITY PRESS

1982

Oxford University Press, Walton Street, Oxford OX2 6DP

London Glasgow New York Toronto
Delhi Bombay Calcutta Madras Karachi
Kuala Lumpur Singapore Hong Kong Tokyo
Nairobi Dar es Salaam Cape Town
Melbourne Auckland

and associate companies in
Beirut Berlin Ibadan Mexico City

© *Brian Davies 1982*

British Library Cataloguing in Publication Data
Davies, Brian
An introduction to the philosophy of religion. – (OPUS)
1. Religion – Philosophy
I. Title II. Series
200'.1 BL51
ISBN 0-19-219158-6
ISBN 0-19-289145-6 Pbk

Set by Filmtype Services Ltd.
Printed in Great Britain
at the University Press, Oxford
by Eric Buckley
Printer to the University

For Dan Williams, Illtyd Trethowan, and Simon Tugwell

Contents

Acknowledgements

A number of people have been kind enough to comment on material which has found its way into this book. In particular I must thank Simon Tugwell, O.P., Hugh Price, Hugo Meynell, Illtyd Trethowan, Stephen Salter, K.V. Wilkes, Alan Ryan, and Herbert McCabe, O.P. I am grateful to Malcolm McMahon, O.P., for compiling the index, and to Henry Hardy and the Oxford University Press for various useful critical reflections.

Blackfriars
Oxford
June 1981

Introduction

It is difficult to say exactly what the philosophy of religion is. One might define it as 'philosophizing about religion'; but there is considerable disagreement over the nature of both philosophy and religion, so even this definition has its drawbacks. The philosophy of religion is now a recognized branch of philosophy, but it would be rash to conclude from this that the philosophy of religion is something unique; that it is, for example, a discipline distinguishable from others as chemistry is from needlework.

In this book I do not attempt the perilous task of defining the philosophy of religion. My intention is to look at some of the topics traditionally thought to fall within its scope. The most prominent of these is the existence of God, so much of what follows is devoted to the question of God's existence. I also deal with the relationship between morality and religion, the concept of miracle, and the notion of life after death. It is inevitable that my own views about certain questions will become clear as the book proceeds, for it is hard to discuss any philosophical issue without taking sides. But I have tried to write about things in a way that should enable the reader to take up some sides for himself. I have also tried to write on the assumption that the reader has little or no philosophical background.

I ought to point out that a great deal more than I discuss could be brought in under the heading of philosophy of religion. There are, for example, topics arising from the comparative study of religion and from various beliefs peculiar to particular religions. But a complete treatise on the philosophy of religion would be a vast and complicated artefact, and space is limited in an introduction. In any case, one has to start somewhere.

It might be helpful to say an additional word at the outset about the structure of what follows. Suppose I ask you to believe that something or other is the case. You can then put two questions to me. First, you can ask whether what I think to be so *could* be so. Then you can ask why you should think (what reason there is to believe) that it is so. For affirmations can be *possibly* true and *actually* true, and they can only be actually true if they are possibly true. This book is very much concerned with questions about possibility and actuality. I frequently ask whether certain views can be immediately ruled out as nonsensical, and then I ask whether there is any reason for accepting them. This method of inquiry is largely dictated by the way in which many religious assertions have recently been dealt with by philosophers. These have often said that certain religious beliefs (especially the belief that there is a God) cannot possibly be true whatever reasons are offered for accepting them. This line of argument clearly needs to be looked at. As I shall maintain, however, it is also open to question, which means that it is legitimate to ask whether certain religious beliefs are capable of rational support. I shall suggest that some are.

A final point. The philosopher of religion can belong to any religion or none, and even if he can show that some religious beliefs are true, it does not follow that he has demonstrated the truth of an entire religious system. One can, for example, believe in God without being committed to religions like Judaism or Christianity. There are numerous theological positions of which I say nothing in this book; so I shall not here be arguing either for or against any particular religion.

1 Verification and falsification

Is there a God? Are there reasons for thinking that God exists? Can God's existence be proved? These questions have greatly interested philosophers of religion, and they are often asked by people who would not regard themselves as professional philosophers. But are they really worth raising at all?

It has been said that they are not. Why? Because the assertion that God exists is either meaningless or else so problematic that there is little point in asking whether it is actually true, or how one can know or reasonably believe it to be so. This suggestion has been particularly prevalent in the twentieth century and it has done much to influence the present state of philosophy of religion. One of its best-known forms holds that there just could not be a God, that 'God exists' is meaningless, since the existence of God is unverifiable or unfalsifiable or both. Let us therefore begin to look at the philosophy of religion by turning to this view.

Verification and belief in God

One can begin to understand it by noting the work of a famous group of philosophers who, in the nineteen-twenties, began to gather in Vienna around a writer called Moritz Schlick (1882–1936). The group became known as the Vienna Circle and it included, among others, Otto Neurath (1882–1945), Friedrich Waismann (1896–1959), and Rudolf Carnap (1891–1970). These men were influenced by Ludwig Wittgenstein (1889–1951), from whom they claimed to derive a theory of meaning known as the Verification Principle. From this they drew drastic and far-reaching conclusions.

The history of philosophy yields much reference to metaphysics, something traditionally understood to include the key claims of religious believers. But the Vienna Circle maintained that all metaphysical assertions are nonsensical. Since traditional metaphysical assertions include religious assertions, the conclusion drawn was that religious assertions are meaningless.

Even with its original exponents the verification principle was stated in different forms and credited with different statuses. Normally, however, it is said to hold that the meaning of a statement is its method of verification. Roughly speaking, the ideas involved in this view are as follows.

Meaningful statements fall into two groups. First, there are mathematical statements, tautologies (e.g. 'All cats are cats'), and logically necessary statements (e.g. 'If all men are mortal and if Socrates is a man, then Socrates is mortal'). Second, there are statements which can be confirmed through the use of human senses, and especially through the methods used in sciences like physics, chemistry, and biology. To ask whether a statement is meaningful is thus to ask if its truth can be confirmed by means of sense experience.

In this way, then, the Vienna Circle tried to locate sense and meaning along with experience. And in doing so it stood in a definite philosophical tradition. Effectively it was agreeing with the Scottish philosopher David Hume (1711–76). 'If', says Hume, 'we take in our hand any volume; of divinity or school metaphysics, for instance, let us ask, *Does it contain any abstract reasoning concerning quantity or number?* No. *Does it contain any experimental reasoning concerning matter of fact and existence?* No. Commit it then to the flames: for it can contain nothing but sophistry and illusion.'[1]

The verification principle became the most distinctive doctrine of Logical Positivism, which is what the school of thinking represented and influenced by the Vienna Circle came to be called. As I have said, however, the principle was not always stated in the same way. Some early formulations take it as a principle about propositions; later ones refer to 'statements' and 'sentences'. A distinction was also made between what has been called the 'weak' and 'strong' versions of the verification principle. The weak version became the most popular. It held that a statement is meaningful if sense experience can go at least some way to confirming it. But in the early days of logical positivism it was the strong version of the verification principle that was in vogue. Waismann stated it thus: 'Anyone uttering a sentence must know under what conditions he calls it true and under what conditions he calls it false. If he is unable to state these conditions, he does not know what he has said. A statement which cannot be conclusively verified cannot be verified at all. It is simply devoid of any meaning.'[2] On Waismann's account, if S is a cognitively meaningful statement there must be a finite and consistent set of observation statements O1 ... On, where S entails and is entailed by putting together O1 ... On. Carnap has a similar principle. He argues that 'it is certain that a sequence of words has a meaning only if its relations of deducibility to the protocol sentences are fixed.'[3] 'Protocol sentences' are supposed to be simple sentences about what is given in experience. They were also called 'observation sentences' or 'basic propositions'.

The history of the verification principle is too complicated for us to follow in detail here, but we can note that all its proponents held that the principle's implications were devastating for belief in God. Take, for example, Carnap. 'In its metaphysical use', he observes, 'the word "God" refers to something beyond experience. The word is deliberately divested of its reference to a physical being or to a spiritual being that is immanent in the physical. And as it is not given a new meaning, it becomes meaningless.'[4] Another illustration of logical positivist methods of dealing with the existence of God (a particularly famous one as it happens) can be found in A. J. Ayer's book *Language, Truth and Logic*.[5] 'The term "god" ', says Ayer, 'is a metaphysical term. And if "god" is a metaphysical term, then it cannot even be probable that a god exists. For to say that "God exists" is to make a metaphysical utterance which cannot be either true or false. And by the same criterion, no sentence which purports to describe the nature of a transcendent god can possess any literal significance.'[6] Note that Ayer is not just denying the existence of God in this passage: he is dismissing the question of God's existence altogether.

Falsification

At this point some thinking related to that just noted ought briefly to be mentioned. Here one can introduce the name of Antony Flew, with whom the emphasis changes from verification to falsification. According to the verification principle, religious statements, including 'There is a God', are meaningless simply because it is not possible to verify them. Flew does not support the principle in this form, but in 'Theology and Falsification'[7] he does ask whether certain religious statements might not be suspect because no sense experience counts against them.

Flew begins by relating what he calls a 'parable'. A and B come upon a clearing in the jungle. A maintains that there is an invisible gardener who looks after it; B denies this suggestion. Various tests (such as keeping watch, using bloodhounds and electric fences) are applied to check whether there is a gardener. All the tests fail to show the gardener's presence, but A continues to maintain his existence. He says, 'But there is a gardener who has no scent and makes no sound, a gardener who comes secretly to look after the garden which he loves.'[8] The sceptic rejects this move and suggests that there is no difference between the believer's gardener and no gardener at all.

At this point Flew applies his parable to religious statements. Religious believers make claims; they say, for instance, that there is a God who loves mankind. But apparently they are unwilling to allow anything to count against these claims. The claims seem unfalsifiable. Are they, then, genuine? Flew does not dogmatically declare that they cannot be, but evidently he has his doubts. 'Sophisticated religious people', he says, 'tend to refuse to allow, not merely that anything actually does occur, but that anything conceivably could occur, which would count against their theological assertions and explanations. But in so far as they do this their supposed explanations are actually bogus, and their seeming assertions are really vacuous.'[9] Flew does not talk in this passage about falsification by sense experience, but it seems reasonable to suppose that this is what he has in mind. The tests which he mentions for checking the gardener's presence could all be called 'sensory'. And from Flew's example of the gardener it should be fairly clear that in raising the issue of falsification he has the question of God's existence pretty much in mind. He seems to be suggesting that those who believe in God are unwilling to allow any sense experience to count against their belief, and he seems to be wondering whether this does not invalidate it.

Verification, falsification, and God

The question we obviously have to ask now is this: is the statement that there is a God meaningless because it is unverifiable or unfalsifiable?

It is clear, to begin with, that we often do regard verification and falsification as ways of distinguishing sense from nonsense. If I say that my dog is a brilliant philosopher you will rightly doubt whether I am talking any sense at all until I am able to show you something about the dog's behaviour that might help to give meaning to my assertion. And you would be justly and similarly sceptical if (a) I say on Tuesday that it will rain on Wednesday, (b) by Thursday it has not rained, and (c) on Thursday I insist that I was right on Tuesday.

It is one thing to say all this, however, and quite another to agree that the writers so far introduced in this chapter say anything to establish that there could not be a God. And when we critically examine what they do say it soon becomes clear that we cannot plausibly use it in defence of such a conclusion.

Take first the view that a statement is only meaningful and factual if it is conclusively verifiable or falsifiable by means of sense experience. This view falls into difficulties when we remember that it seems possible to make intelligible and factual universal statements like 'All men spend part of their lives asleep' or 'All cats are mortal'. The first statement here is, as far as we know, true. Yet there is no way in which one could conclusively show that it is true by means of sense experience. This is because it is always possible that one will one day come across a man who needs no sleep at all. As for the second statement, that too seems true. But it cannot be conclusively falsified. For however old the cats of one's experience may be, they may die one day. Therefore, it is wrong to appeal to conclusive verifiability and falsifiability as criteria of meaningfulness for factual statements.

It might, however, be argued that the weak version of the verification principle is still useful and that this can serve to establish the impossibility of God's existence once and for all. But this view is open to the initial objection that the weak principle does not even satisfy its own criterion of meaningfulness. If one accepts it, one would have to say that a statement is only factual and meaningful if some sense experience or observation statement makes it probable or counts in its favour. But what sense experience or observation statement can count in favour of the claim that a statement is only factual and meaningful if some sense experience or observation statement makes it probable or counts in its favour?

It has been urged that the verification principle is acceptable because it only takes up the ordinary understanding of words like 'factual' and 'meaningful'. Schlick, for example, said that it is 'nothing but a simple statement of the way in which meaning is actually assigned to propositions in everyday life and in science. There never has been any other way, and it would be a grave error to suppose that we have discovered a new conception of meaning which is contrary to common opinion and which we want to introduce into philosophy.'[10] But this remark seems to overlook the fact that many people apparently regard as meaningful and factual a whole lot of statements which do not seem confirmable only by means of sense experience. Take, for example, religious people and the way they regard as both factual and meaningful statements about God and life after death. And to this point one can add another. Consider the following statement given as an example by Richard Swinburne: 'Some of the toys which to all appearances stay in the toy cupboard while people are asleep and no one is watching, actually get up and dance in the middle of the night and then go back to the cupboard leaving no traces of their activity.'[11] Now if someone were to say this, talking, let us suppose, about a particular cupboard, we might be utterly incredulous. Swinburne's example is a frivolous one. But it would be stretching things to say that the statement he asks us to consider is meaningless, that it could be neither true nor false. It might be replied that no one could understand a statement unless he knew how it could be shown to be true or false. It might be added that knowing how to show a statement true or false means knowing what available sense experience would make it either probable or improbable. But people also seem able to understand statements without being able to say what available sense experience would make it likely or unlikely that they are true. To take another example of Swinburne:

A man can understand the statement 'once upon a time, before there were men or any other rational creatures, the earth was covered by sea', without his having any idea of what geological evidence would count for or against this proposition, or any idea of how to establish what geological evidence would count for or against the proposition.[12]

The truth of this observation is just what someone could well refer to if it were said that Antony Flew's comments about falsifiability made it obvious that statements about God are clearly meaningless. Someone who says that there is a God might not be able to specify what exactly would count against the truth of his assertion. But it does not follow from this that the assertion is meaningless.

Must we then conclude that the verification principle is thoroughly misguided? I have already offered reasons for rejecting it, but it is worth noting in conclusion that even a vigorous proponent of it can be forced to go back on his approval. To illustrate the point we can turn again to A. J. Ayer.

In the first edition of *Language, Truth and Logic* Ayer attempted to state a version of the weak form of the verification principle. He took the expression 'experiential proposition' to mean any proposition which reports a possible or actual observation. Then he suggested that 'it is the mark of a genuine factual proposition not that it should be equivalent to an experiential proposition, or any finite number of experiential propositions, but simply that some experiential propositions can be deduced from it in conjunction with certain other premises without being deducible from these other premises alone.'[13] But, as Ayer himself came to see, this statement of the verification principle is not adequate at all. For it would allow that any purported statement at all is meaningful. Take any purported statement, S, and take any 'experiential proposition', E. On Ayer's criterion quoted above we can show that S is meaningful since E follows from S and 'If S then E', while E does not follow from 'If S then E' alone.

In recognizing the force of this difficulty Ayer reformulated the verification principle. In the second edition of *Language, Truth and Logic* he wrote:

I propose to say that a statement is indirectly verifiable if it satisfies the following conditions: first, that in conjunction with certain other premises it entails one or more directly verifiable statements which are not deducible from these other premises alone; and secondly, that these other premises do not include any statement that is not either analytic, or directly verifiable, or capable of being independently established as indirectly verifiable. And I can now reformulate the principle of verification as requiring of a literally meaningful statement, which is not analytic, that it should be either directly or indirectly verifiable, in the foregoing sense.[14]

But is this reformulation successful? Unfortunately not.

According to Ayer, a statement is directly verifiable 'if it is either itself an observation statement or is such that in conjunction with one or more observation statements it entails at least one observation statement which is not deducible from these other premises alone'.[15] Consider, now, three observation statements, 01, 02, and 03, none of which entails any of the others by itself. Take also a purported statement of any kind, for example 'There is a God', and call it S. Consider, now, the following:

Either (Not-01 and 02) or (03 and not-S).

This statement is directly verifiable according to Ayer as quoted above. For, together with 01, it gives 03, while 03 is not entailed by 01 alone. Thus:

Either (Not-01 and 02) or (03 and not-S)
01
Therefore 03.

If now one puts

Either (Not-01 and 02) or (03 and not-S)

together with S one gets:

Either (Not-01 and 02) or (03 and not-S)
S
Therefore 02.

So S is indirectly verifiable according to Ayer's new criterion. And any statement whatever, including one like 'There is a God', can be shown to be meaningful in terms of Ayer's restatement of the verification principle.

Ayer now admits this point himself. In *The Central Questions of Philosophy*[16] he considers the above argument (which originates with Alonzo Church)[17] and he accepts it. He also indicates that if Not-03 is substituted for 01 in

Either (Not-01 and 02) or (03 and not-S)

then the above argument would count against a criterion of meaning stated in terms of falsification. It would show that any statement whatever is falsifiable and that, for example, a statement like 'There is a God' is falsifiable and therefore meaningful.

So the verification principle in the forms in which we have considered it does not show that there could not be a God. Nor does it seem that God's existence has to be ruled out because it cannot be falsified. But might there not be other reasons for holding that there could not be a God? In the next chapter we will consider this question with reference to a problem often discussed by philosophers of religion. It centres on the possibility of talking significantly about God in the light of the way people normally speak about him. More precisely, it springs from the fact that talk about God seems to pull in two different directions.

2 Talking about God

'I love you', says the lady. 'Do you really mean that?', asks her boy friend. 'No', the lady replies. The boy friend is speechless, and not without reason. The lady seems to be saying nothing significant. What she gives with one hand she takes back with the other.

Some people have felt that those who believe in God are rather like the lady just referred to, and, in their view, this means that belief in God raises an insurmountable problem for anyone who supposes that one can reasonably be asked to look at any defence of the view that there actually is a God.

This problem derives from two facts. The first is that God is typically spoken of as if he could be compared with various things with which we are already familiar. The second is that God is typically said to be very different from anything that comes within the range of our experience. On the one hand, God is said to be, for example, good or wise. On the other, he is said to be unique in a very strong sense and our talk of him, so it is said, fails to do him justice. God is good, but not in the way that anything else is. God is wise, but not in the way that Solomon was wise.

Here, then, is the problem. If one says that God is very different from anything else, can one really talk significantly about him at all? How can one say that God is good or wise but not in the sense that ordinary good and wise things are? Is there not a real dilemma here for those who believe in God? Are they not caught between the stools of meaninglessness and misrepresentation?

Negation and analogy

Defenders of belief in God have not been unaware of the force of such questions and they have consequently tried to say how one can talk significantly about God without also misrepresenting him. In particular they have frequently appealed to the importance of negation and analogy.

The appeal to negation is easy to understand and is best thought of as an attempt to prevent people from misrepresenting God. It emphasizes the unknowability of God and argues that though one can talk significantly about God one can only do so by saying what God is not. A notable advocate of negation is Maimonides (1135–1204), who writes as follows:

There is no necessity at all for you to use positive attributes of God with the view of magnifying Him in your thoughts ... I will give you ... some illustrations, in order that you may better understand the propriety of forming as many negative attributes as possible, and the impropriety of ascribing to God any positive attributes. A person may know for certain that a 'ship' is in existence, but he may not know to what object that name is applied, whether to a substance or to an accident; a second person then learns that a ship is not an accident; a third, that it is not a mineral; a fourth, that it is not a plant growing in the earth; a fifth, that it is not a body whose parts are joined together by nature; a sixth, that it is not a flat object like boards or doors; a seventh, that it is not a sphere; an eighth, that it is not pointed; a ninth, that it is not round shaped; nor equilateral; a tenth, that it is not solid. It is clear that this tenth person has almost arrived at the correct notion of a 'ship' by the foregoing negative attributes. ... In the same manner you will come nearer to the knowledge and comprehension of God by the negative attributes. ... I do not merely declare that he who affirms attributes of God has not sufficient knowledge concerning the Creator ... but I say that he unconsciously loses his belief in God.[1]

So much, then, for the notion of talking about God by means of negation. Historically speaking, however, it is analogy that has most interested those who agree that even a unique God can be spoken about significantly. In this connection it is even possible to speak about 'the theory of analogy'. In order to say what that is, it will help if I go back to the problem with which we started and introduce some new terminology.

It seems that words applied to God cannot bear exactly the same senses when they are applied to God and to creatures. But must there not be something similar said when, for example, it is said both that some man is good and that God is good? To put it another way, can one only apply a word to God and to other things either *univocally* or *equivocally*? To apply a word univocally to two things is to say that they are exactly the same in some respect, that the word means the same in both its applications. Thus I might say that Paris and Rome are both cities, and here I would be using the word 'city' univocally. To apply words equivocally, however, is to use the same words in completely different senses. We would be using the word 'bat' equivocally if we used it to refer both to the little furry mammals and to the things used by cricketers.

Now according to the theory of analogy, there is a third way of applying the same word to different things, and this fact is important when we are thinking about the way in which one may talk about God. The idea is that one can use words analogically. The analogical use of words is supposed to lie somewhere between the univocal and the equivocal.

We can see the theory of analogy classically applied to God in the work of Thomas Aquinas (1224/5–74) who explicitly raises the question, 'Are words used univocally or equivocally of God and creatures?'[2] His answer runs as follows.

The same term cannot be applied to God and creatures univocally. When, for example, we call creatures 'wise' we are saying that they possess a certain attribute. And when we say this we have to allow that the attribute in question is distinct from other attributes and even from the fact of there being anything to possess it. In the case of God, however, we cannot distinguish his attributes from each other; nor can we distinguish them from his very existence (in Aquinas's language, from his *esse*). So we have to agree that when an attribute is ascribed to God, when it is said, for example, 'God is wise', what the attribute word 'signifies in God is not confined to the meaning of our word but goes beyond it. Hence it is clear that the word "wise" is not used in the same sense of God and man, and the same is true of all other words, so they cannot be used univocally of God and creatures.'[3]

On the other hand, words applied to God cannot always be used equivocally. As Aquinas puts it, if we always used words equivocally when talking about God, 'we could never argue from statements about creatures to statements about God.'[4]

Aquinas thus concludes that 'words are used of God and creatures in an analogical way.' Here Aquinas distinguishes two kinds of analogical language. On the one hand, we can apply a word, W, to two things, A and B, because of some relationship in which A and B stand to some other thing to which we can also apply W. Thus we can call a diet and a complexion 'healthy', and we can call a man 'healthy'. The diet is healthy because it causes a man to be healthy; the complexion is healthy because it is a symptom of health. We can also apply the same word to two things because they have some relation to each other. Thus we can call a diet and a man 'healthy' because the diet causes the man to be healthy. In the case of God, Aquinas concludes, terms are applied analogically because of some relation between God and creatures. And the relation which Aquinas has in mind is causal. Perfections that creatures have can be said to exist in God in that he is the cause of creatures.

In this way some words are used neither univocally nor purely equivocally of God and creatures, but analogically, for we cannot speak of God at all except in the language we use of creatures, and so whatever is said both of God and creatures is said in virtue of the order that creatures have to God as to their source and cause in which all perfections of things pre-exist transcendently.[5]

Negation, analogy, and God

What, then, shall we say of all this? Does the appeal to negation and analogy serve to allay the doubt that reasons for belief in God are just not worth looking at? Given the way that people talk of God, is the question of his existence a real non-starter? Are writers like Maimonides and Aquinas simply wasting our time?

In fairness to Maimonides and to those who agree with him it ought at least to be said that talking of God by means of negation has some justification once one reflects on the way in which God has been understood within the Judaeo-Christian tradition. God has regularly been thought of as the Creator, as the source of all things. As Aquinas puts it, 'The word "God" signifies the divine nature: it is used to mean something that is above all that is, and that is the source of all things and is distinct from them all. This is how those that use it mean it to be used.'[6] To talk of God can readily be regarded as to talk about whatever it is that all particular beings depend on in so far as they exist, in so far as they are there rather than not there, in so far, indeed, as there is anywhere for them to be. And this point, which is certainly obscure, also seems important. For once we agree that God is the source of all things, it seems plausible to conclude that he cannot himself be a thing and that saying that God is not this and not that is the only alternative open to us if we are not to talk out-and-out nonsense about God. We cannot literally mean that the Creator is *a* this or *a* that.

But the position that one can talk significantly about God only by means of negations is still difficult to defend. Here there are at least two points to note.

The first concerns the claim that it is possible to approach some understanding of God simply by saying what God is not. Maimonides evidently thinks that this claim is true; but the reverse is the case. For only saying what something is not gives no indication of what it actually is, and if one can only say what God is not, one cannot understand him at all. Suppose I say that there is something in my room, and suppose I reject every suggestion you make as to what is actually there. In that case, you will get no idea at all about what is in my room. Going back to the quotation from Maimonides on p.10, it is simply unreasonable to say that someone who has all the negations mentioned in it 'has almost arrived at the correct notion of a "ship"'. He could equally well be thinking of a wardrobe.

The second point is that people who talk about God do not normally want to talk about him only in negations. They usually want to say that some things are definitely true of him. It has been suggested that one can understand talk of God in such a way that it should always be construed as talk of something else. In this way it has been urged that what look like positive statements about God are really nothing of the kind. But this suggestion does not seem to square with a great deal that is said about God. When, for example, people who believe in God say that he is good, they normally mean that God really is good and not that something is true of some being other than God.

If a rigid reliance on negation is not without its drawbacks, the theory of analogy is more promising. For there is a lot to be said for the view that the same word can be applied to different things neither univocally nor equivocally. This point can be illustrated by quoting a useful passage at the beginning of Wittgenstein's *Philosophical Investigations*.

Consider for example the proceedings that we call 'games'. I mean board-games, card-games, ball-games, Olympic games, and so on. What is common to them all? – Don't say: 'There *must* be something common, or they would not be called "games" ' – but *look and see* whether there is anything common to them all. – For if you look at them you will not see something that is common to *all*, but similarities, relationships, and a whole series of them at that. To repeat: don't think, but look! – Look for example at board-games, with their multifarious relationships. Now pass to card-games; here you find many correspondences with the first group, but many common features drop out, and others appear. When we pass next to ball-games, much that is common is retained, but much is lost. – Are they all 'amusing'? Compare chess with noughts and crosses. Or is there always winning and losing, or competition between players? Think of patience. . . . And we can go through the many, many other groups of games in the same way; can see how similarities crop up and disappear.[7]

What Wittgenstein brings out very clearly is that at least one word can significantly be used in different but related senses. And, following the clue offered by his example, we can quickly come to see that many words can significantly be used in this way. Take, for instance, 'good'. You can have good food and good books, not to mention good people, good wine, and a good night's sleep. Or again, there is Aquinas's illustration, the word 'healthy'. As Aquinas says, a man can be healthy, and so can a complexion or a diet. In saying that a man, a complexion, and a diet are healthy one is not saying that they are exactly alike in some respect. But nor is one saying that they are different as mammalian bats are different from wooden ones.

It seems wrong, then, to hold that the same words must always bear exactly the same meaning or be used on some occasions in ways that are non-significant and therefore that nobody can talk significantly about God since words applied to him do not mean exactly what they do when applied to other things. To put it another way, the problem raised at the beginning of this chapter is not obviously insurmountable; just because people do not apply words to God and to creatures either univocally or equivocally it does not follow that they cannot talk about God in any significant way. That is what the theory of analogy is basically saying, and in this it is surely right.

But we are still left with a difficulty. Even if we grant that the univocal/equivocal distinction can be supplemented, we can still ask why particular words are used in talking about God and whether they are capable of being used significantly. We may accept that the word 'game' can be used to describe things which do not have a common feature, but we would also agree that not just anything can be called a game. Rescuing a drowning child is not a game; nor is performing a surgical operation. So there is still a general problem for talk about God. Some reason must be given for choosing the terms which are actually applied to God. This point is nicely put by Patrick Sherry who suggests that:

It is not just a matter of saying that there must be some grounds for ascribing perfections to God. We must also insist that if we ascribe the same terms to God and creatures, then there must be a connection between the relevant criteria of evidence and truth. Thus the grounds for ascribing terms like 'love', 'father', 'exist' and 'life' must bear some relationship to the grounds used for our normal everyday application of these terms. Similarly, even if 'God created the world' expresses a unique relationship, its truth conditions must bear some resemblance to our familiar uses of terms like 'make' or 'depends on' (which is not to say that we must expect to be able to verify the doctrine of Creation empirically here and now).[8]

So the terms used in talking about God must be justified in some way if they are not to appear arbitrary and empty of meaning. But the question is, can they be? Aquinas, for example, thought that they can. He held that one can come to a knowledge of God and one can significantly apply to God words which apply to creatures because there is some positive reason for doing so. But is Aquinas right in adopting this position? Could anybody be right in adopting it?

At this stage in the discussion it is difficult to say, for we have not yet touched on any particular reasons for believing in God and affirming anything of him. For the moment, however, this does not matter. In this chapter we have been asking whether reasons for belief in God are even worth looking at in view of some things that are said of him. For all we have seen so far, the answer is Yes.

In the next chapter we shall consider a problem which has led many people to a different conclusion. Before moving on, however, it is worth briefly making a final point. Even from what we have seen already, it should be clear enough that people who believe in God seem committed to thinking of him as something decidedly out of the ordinary. Some would say that he is essentially mysterious. But does this mean that he could not exist? And does it mean that there could never be reasons for belief in God?

Affirmative answers have been offered to both these questions. It has been suggested that if God is really mysterious, then we cannot understand exactly what is being said when he is talked about, in which case it is nonsense to affirm his existence. It has also been said that if God is really mysterious, then it is pointless to try and find reasons for holding that he exists.

But these views are not very plausible. One does not have to know exactly what a word means in order to have some understanding of it or in order to use it significantly. I may not know what a volcano is exactly, but I can still talk sensibly about volcanoes. And I can reasonably say that Jones has malaria without being clear as to what exactly I am saying. In other words, I can wield words significantly without being able to define them. As Peter Geach puts it, 'I certainly could not define either "oak-tree" or "elephant"; but this does not destroy my right to assert that no oak-tree is an elephant.'[9] This point does nothing to show that there is a God, but it does suggest that in order to speak meaningfully about God it is not necessary that one should understand exactly the import of one's statements about him. It may not be possible to define God; one may not be able fully to comprehend him. But this does not mean that one cannot significantly talk about him; nor does it prevent one from asking whether he is there in the first place.

3 God and evil

As some philosophers would put it, the questions considered in the last two chapters involve the *a priori* possibility of God's existence. They are concerned with the intrinsic possibility of God's existence, with whether there *could* be a God. One outcome of our discussion so far is that it is advisable to ask whether there is any reason to believe in God, and in Chapter 4 we will begin to do just this by turning to one of a series of arguments for God's existence. First, however, I want to consider what many people regard as the clearest indication that there could not be a God. I refer to what is commonly called 'the problem of evil', something that has been discussed for centuries.

What is the problem of evil?

The problem of evil is usually understood as a problem for *classical theism* (sometimes just called *theism*), supporters of which are commonly called *theists*. As H. P. Owen puts it in his book *Concepts of Deity*, 'Theism may be defined as belief in one God, the Creator, who is infinite, self-existent, incorporeal, eternal, immutable, impassible, simple, perfect, omniscient and omnipotent.'[1] Some of the terms in Owen's definition are technical ones and do not require explanation at this point. We shall be coming back to many of them later. For the moment, however, we can at least note three things. First, to say that God is omniscient is to say that he is all-knowing. Second, to call God omnipotent is to say that he is all-powerful. Third, to say that God is perfect is in part to mean that he is all-good.

According to classical theism, then, God is all-knowing, all-powerful, and all-good. In the world around us, however, we discover varieties of evil which can, in fact, be roughly divided into two kinds. These have traditionally been called 'metaphysical evil' and 'moral evil'. Metaphysical evil (also called 'natural evil') is all that we regard as evil in the physical universe, all that cannot plausibly be regarded as resulting from the free choices of human agents. Sickness and natural disasters would fall into the category of metaphysical evil. Moral evil, on the other hand, is usually regarded as morally culpable behaviour. When Jones tortures Brown just for the fun of it, and realizing that his action is wrong, he would be said to illustrate what is meant by moral evil. Sometimes, of course, the two kinds of evil overlap. I might deliberately arrange for someone to be in a place where I know he will be killed by a typhoon. But moral and metaphysical evil can still, for the sake of argument, be distinguished. Metaphysical evil could still be there even if human beings always behaved perfectly.

Now the problem of evil is commonly seen as the problem of how the existence of God and the existence of evil are to be reconciled. And it has often been said that they cannot be. Thus it has been urged that the problem of evil constitutes grounds for disbelief in God. The argument here has taken two forms. First, it has been said that given the existence of evil it is most reasonable to conclude that there is no God. Second, and more directly relevant to us at this stage in our discussion, it has been held that because of the existence of evil the theist is caught in a contradiction. He cannot say *both* that there is evil *and* that God exists. Since he can hardly deny that there is evil, it follows that God does not exist. As St. Augustine (354–430) puts it: 'Either God cannot abolish evil or He will not; if He cannot then He is not all-powerful; if He will not then He is not all-good.'[2] In Aquinas's formulation: 'It seems that there is no God. For if, of two mutually exclusive things, one were to exist without limit, the other would cease to exist. But by the word "God" is implied limitless good. If, then, God existed, nobody would ever encounter evil. But evil is encountered in the world. God therefore does not exist.'[3]

Some notable responses to the problem of evil

Theists have often acknowledged that the problem of evil raises a difficulty for them; so we can now turn to some of the ways in which they have attempted to deal with it.

One very common line of argument is that the existence of some evil is a necessary means to some good. One version of this argument can be found in Richard Swinburne's book *The Existence of God*.[4] According to Swinburne natural evil provides, among other things, an opportunity for people to grow in knowledge and understanding. He writes:

If men are to have knowledge of the evil which will result from their actions or negligence, laws of nature must operate regularly; and that means that there will be what I may call 'victims of the system' . . . *if* men are to have the opportunity to bring about serious evils for themselves or others by actions or negligence, or to prevent their occurrence, and if all knowledge of the future is obtained by normal induction, that is by induction from patterns of similar events in the past – then there must be serious natural evils occurring to man or animals.[5]

Swinburne considers the possibility of God giving men the necessary knowledge by somehow informing them of the way things are and what they can do about it. He suggests that God might inform mankind verbally about such matters. But according to Swinburne this would mean that nobody could fail to doubt God's existence and everyone would be forced to accept God and to act as he wished. Furthermore, nobody would be able to choose to acquire knowledge of the world for himself. 'I conclude', says Swinburne,

that a world in which God gave to men verbal knowledge of the consequences of their actions would not be a world in which men had a significant choice of destiny, of what to make of themselves, and of the world. God would be far too close for them to be able to work things out for themselves. If God is to give man knowledge while at the same time allowing him a genuine choice of destiny, it must be normal inductive knowledge.[6]

A related view can be found in the work of John Hick, one of the most prominent contemporary writers on the problem of evil. He argues that the existence of evil is necessary for the perfect development of human beings. Hick understands evil in the light of God's desire not to coerce people into accepting him. He suggests that man is a sin-prone creature, created as such by God, but able, in a world containing evil, to rise to great heights because he is given the opportunity to become mature in the face of evil. He writes:

My general conclusion, then, is that this world with all its unjust and apparently wasted suffering, may nevertheless be what the Irenaean strand of Christian thought affirms that it is, namely a divinely created sphere of soul-making.... Let us suppose that the infinite personal God creates finite persons to share in the life which He imparts to them. If He creates them in his immediate presence, so that they cannot fail to be conscious from the first of the infinite divine being and glory, goodness and love, wisdom, power and knowledge in whose presence they are, they will have no creaturely independence in relation to their Maker. They will not be able to *choose* to worship God, or to turn to Him freely as valuing spirits responding to infinite Value. In order, then, to give them the freedom to come to Him, God creates them at a distance – not a spatial but an epistemic distance. He causes them to come into a situation in which He is not immediately and overwhelmingly evident to them. Accordingly they come to self-consciousness as parts of a universe which has its own autonomous structures and 'laws'.... A world without problems, difficulties, perils, and hardships would be morally static. For moral and spiritual growth comes through response to challenges; and in a paradise there would be no challenges. Accordingly, a person-making environment cannot be plastic to human wishes but must have its own structure in terms of which men have to learn to live and which they ignore at their peril.[7]

Notice how much emphasis is placed in this argument on human freedom. Such an emphasis is the main feature of another famous response to the problem of evil – the free-will defence, which tries to show that God's existence is compatible with moral evil. It can be stated roughly as follows.

Much evil can be attributed to human agents. This evil need never have occurred, but if there is to be a world of free human agents, it must be possible for these agents to bring about moral evil. If they were thwarted in doing so they would not be really free. Now it is better that there should be a world containing free agents than that there should be a world full of robots or automata. In creating people, therefore, God was faced with an alternative. He could either have created a world lacking moral evil, or he could have created a world where moral evil was a genuine possibility. If he had created the former he could not have created a world containing free agents. In fact, he created the latter, and this means that there is a genuine and unavoidable possibility of moral evil. In creating the world he did create God was making the better choice. For a world containing free agents is better than a world without them. Hence God is good, even though he permits people to bring about all sorts of moral evil, and the existence of God is compatible with the existence of evil.

Evil, consequences, and freedom

But do the above responses show that there could be a God in spite of the evil that exists? Or must we conclude that the problem of evil renders God's existence impossible or unlikely?

Turning first to the kind of argument represented by Swinburne and Hick, there is at least one sense in which it seems unsuccessful. The issue here turns on the question of actions and consequences.

Both Swinburne and Hick think of God's goodness as moral goodness which can be defended with reference to consequences. They seem to be arguing that when we look at things in a long-term perspective we can regard God as justified in bringing about or allowing various kinds of evil. But is this really so?

We certainly consider that it is often relevant to appeal to consequences in making moral judgements. We also often look favourably on people who bring about evil as a necessary means to a good. Thus we would praise someone for cutting off a man's leg in order to save his life, even if the operation caused great pain to the patient. But many people would say that consequences do not always justify actions, and in the light of this view they have sometimes added that God cannot be excused with reference to consequences for creating a world with the kinds of evil in it that there are. A good representative of this view is D. Z. Phillips.

In Chapter 1 we noted Flew's suggestion that people who believe in God do not seem to allow anything to count against their belief. In making this suggestion Flew speaks of the assertion that God loves us as a father loves his child, and he notes that this assertion seems hard to believe when we are confronted with a child dying of inoperable throat cancer. Swinburne and Hick would presumably reply by appealing to consequences. Swinburne, indeed, will presumably call the child a 'victim of the system'. But Phillips thinks differently. 'What then are we to say of the child dying from cancer?' he asks.[8] The reply is: 'If this has been *done* to anyone, it is bad enough, but to be done for a purpose, to be planned from eternity – that is the deepest evil. If God is this kind of agent, He cannot justify His actions, and His evil nature is revealed.'[9] As Phillips goes on to say, this is the conclusion which Ivan Karamazov reaches in his famous speech to Alyosha in *The Brothers Karamazov*.

And if the sufferings of children go to swell the sum of sufferings which was necessary to pay for truth, then I protest that the truth is not worth such a price. . . . I don't want harmony. From love of humanity I don't want it. . . . Besides, too high a price is asked for harmony; it's beyond our means to pay so much to enter on it. And so I hasten to give back my entrance ticket, and if I am an honest man I am bound to give it back as soon as possible. It's not God that I don't accept, Alyosha, only I most respectfully return Him the ticket.[10]

Now is Phillips wrong in taking the line that he does? It is very hard to see how we are to decide this matter, for what is at stake now is a fundamental moral option, something that Wittgenstein calls an 'absolute judgment of value'.[11] Swinburne and Hick are evidently prepared to allow that consequences can justify bringing about or permitting the evil that exists. Phillips is not. But there seems no way of showing that either side is right or wrong. In that case, however, it seems that Swinburne and Hick cannot say that their view of God and evil is clearly acceptable. If we take the Phillips line, it is clearly misguided; far from exonerating God it only serves to highlight his badness. Someone who agrees with Swinburne and Hick about consequences and evil might be justified in defending God's moral integrity in the light of consequences. But someone who agrees that much of the evil in the world could never be justified by consequences would be bound to reject the Swinburne–Hick defence.

But can we not now appeal to the free-will defence? Does not this show that at least a great deal of evil is compatible with the existence of God? Many people would say that it does and here they would refer to the value we place on freedom. It is a premise of the defence that a world of free agents is better than a world of automata. Most people would accept this premise, and it is certainly true that we normally think well of those who allow their fellow human beings a measure of autonomy and freedom. The oppressive parent and the tyrannical lover, the dictator and the bully, tend to be regarded as less than fully admirable. Might it not therefore be said that if God is really good he could actually be expected to allow his creatures freedom? And then, of course, might it not be said that he could actually be expected to allow them to act as they choose, with all the possible implications for the production of evil that this might imply?

But there is a serious objection to the free-will defence. For the defence assumes that a free act cannot be caused by God. Its proponents have seen this clearly enough. Hence, for example, Alvin Plantinga writes: 'God can create free creatures, but he cannot *cause* or *determine* them to do only what is right. For if he does so, then they are not significantly free after all; they do not do what is right *freely*.'[12] But the assumption that God does not cause free actions is difficult to reconcile with classical theism. For whatever a free act is (and that is a big philosophical question in its own right), it is necessarily an act of somebody. And the notion of somebody acting without being caused to do so by God is hard to accept if we are thinking in terms of classical theism. This holds that God's creative causality is not something exercised in the past. It thinks of it as something that is operative as long as anything apart from God exists at all. Thus we hear it said that everything depends on God for its existence, that the sheer fact of there being anything at all is ultimately due to God's activity, that God is the first cause lying behind all the causal processes that are distinct from his own being. As Owen says:

According to classical theism God created the world 'out of nothing' (*ex nihilo*). Two things must be noted concerning this phrase *ex nihilo*. First, it is analytic, not synthetic. It does not add anything to the idea of creation; it merely makes the idea explicit. Secondly, 'nothing' is to be taken in the strict sense of absolute non-being or non-existence. There is no form of being that exists apart from God's creative act. Everything depends absolutely on him for its very being.[13]

If, then, we are working with the classical theistic view of God we have to agree that if there is a God then he is causally operative in the existence of all things all the time that they exist. But this must mean that he is causally operative in all the actions of human beings, for these too exist in the sense of being actual occurrences. This point seems to have been well grasped by Aquinas. As he puts it, if there is a God,

he is the cause not only of becoming [*quantum ad fieri*] but of being [*quantum ad esse*]. So God can be called the cause of an action in so far as he causes and conserves in being its natural power. . . . But since nothing but an unmoved mover moves or acts of itself, there is [another] sense in which something can be called the cause of another's action – in so far as it moves it to act. . . . God, then, causes the action of every natural thing by moving and applying its power to action.[14]

With commendable consistency, Aquinas even spells out the implication of this view for human wrongdoing, which he calls 'sin'. In the *Summa Theologiae* he asks whether the human action of sinning comes from God (*utrum actus peccati sit a Deo*) and he replies that it does.

The act of sin not only belongs to the realm of being but it is also an act. And from both these points of view it somehow comes from God. Every being, regardless of its manner of existence, must be derived from the First Being, as Dionysius says. Every action is caused by something already in act because moving another to act presupposes that the mover has the power to act. Every being which is in act is reduced to the First Act, i.e. God, as to its cause, Who is act by the very fact of being God. Therefore, in so far as a thing can be called an action, God is its cause.[15]

So the free-will defence is defective. It holds that God merely allows free human actions to take place. But God must be causally involved in their taking place, in which case he does more than just allow them. In some sense he brings them about. Someone who believes in classical theism seems committed to rejecting the free-will defence. But does this mean he cannot defend his view that the problem of evil does not make it unreasonable or impossible to believe in God? I think the answer is No. The reason lies in the nature of the problem of evil and the nature of classical theism.

God and evil

As it is usually presented, the problem of evil is a problem which arises on the assumption that if God exists he must be morally good. Hence it is that writers like Swinburne and Hick try to deal with it by attempting to exonerate God from the moral point of view in spite of the existence of evil. But suppose we now introduce a new question into the discussion. Suppose we ask whether the theist is bound to regard God as a moral agent. Once we do this a whole new line of defence is open to someone who thinks it reasonable to believe in the existence of God along with the existence of evil. For, clearly, if belief in God is not necessarily belief in the existence of a moral agent, then the problem of evil as it has been discussed in this chapter cannot even get off the ground. As some philosophers would put it, it turns into a pseudo-problem. And in that case, of course, it is not necessarily a reason for ignoring any positive case offered for believing in God. For if the problem of evil depends on thinking of God as a moral agent, and if theists do not have to regard Him as such, then the problem is not necessarily a problem for belief in God.

So do we have to say that belief in the existence of God is belief in the existence of a moral agent? If God is thought of as just an extraordinary person, the answer might be affirmative. But within the terms of classical theism it seems more appropriate to reply in the negative.

One reason for saying so is that classical theism thinks of God as the source of all beings. In Owen's words, quoted above, it holds that 'Everything depends absolutely on him for its very being.' But if God is the source of all beings, something has to be done to distinguish him from all beings, and the obvious thing to do is to deny that God is a being. Yet moral agents, whether bad or good, are obviously beings. As we understand them, they are human beings. If God then is not, in terms of classical theism, properly spoken of as a being, he is not properly spoken of as a moral agent. As Michael Durrant argues:

God is said to be the principle of being, which rules 'God' out from being a generic term. On this account, God as the principle of all being, would be that in virtue of which 'exists', which has as many senses as there are categories, can nevertheless be said to be non-homonymous. Hence, God cannot fall under any category, not even 'Substance', as Aquinas points out.[16]

A second reason for denying that classical theism is committed to regarding God as a moral agent brings us to the notions of obligation and duty. It is commonly said that a moral agent is someone able to do his duty, someone capable of living up to his obligations. But it seems very hard to see how the God of classical theism can be thought of as having duties or obligations. These normally confront people in social contexts, in contexts where there are other people around. But, according to classical theism, God is the source of all beings. Furthermore, as Owen points out, classical theism maintains both that 'God's creative act is free in so far as it is neither externally constrained nor necessary for the fulfilment of his own life',[17] and that God is changeless, that, in Owen's words, 'God is incapable of suffering change from either an external or an internal cause.'[18] But if God is the cause of all beings, he must be radically distinct from all that goes to make up and participate in any social context. And if God can be what he is whether or not he creates, if he is free to create, and if he is changeless, he cannot literally be thought of as having a social context and he can be what he is without any such context existing at all. It might be replied that duties and obligations can be binding on people even if they live in total isolation. What about duties and obligations to oneself? But these presuppose being able to do or to refrain from doing something. That is why we do not talk of, for example, having a duty or obligation to be in two places at once, or of being obliged or duty-bound to stop breathing. But if God is changeless, then the notion of his being able to do something or to refrain from doing it makes no sense, at least, not in the way that it would have to for someone who wanted to say that God has obligations or duties to himself. In terms of classical theism God is free to create or not to create, but creation, for the classical theist, cannot involve any change in God.

The notion of God's changelessness means that God just does what he does, or, as some would prefer to say, that he just is what he is.

Lastly, there is the connection between being a moral agent and being able to succeed or fail. A moral agent is obviously one who can in some sense either succeed or fail. He can succeed if he acts morally where others have failed to do so, and he can fail if he acts immorally where others have succeeded. But it makes no sense to talk of the God of classical theism as succeeding or failing. For success and failure are relative to context and are only intelligible in the light of it. One can only be said to have succeeded or failed against a background of success and failure, a background against which one can be judged to have succeeded or failed, a standard against which one's performance can be measured. But if, as classical theism holds, God creates *ex nihilo,* he can have no such background. A man can be judged to have succeeded as a writer in the light of the history of writing. A watch-maker can be judged to have failed as a watch-maker against the background of the history of watch-making. But what is the background for judging the Creator *ex nihilo?* There cannot be any, in which case the God of classical theism cannot be said to be even capable of succeeding or failing. And in that case he cannot be a moral agent, for such an agent must be able either to succeed or to fail.

Reasons for the existence of God?

A great deal more needs to be said about the problem of evil, but I shall now leave the reader with the suggestion that, as it is normally presented, the problem does not rule out the possible existence of God. One may be uncomfortable with the moral premises in positions like those of Swinburne and Hick, but the God of classical theism need not be regarded as a moral agent and cannot therefore be morally bad. When it is referred to as showing the impossibility of God's existence, the problem of evil is normally thought to show that God is morally bad – or, rather, that he would be if he existed, which he cannot since if he did he would be morally bad, which he is not supposed to be. But since the God of classical theism cannot be morally bad, the problem of evil cannot be used to show that he is. As long as we are thinking in terms of classical theism, to say that God is morally bad is rather like saying that pigs are reptilian. To blame him for being morally bad is like criticizing a dog for not having kittens.

Before we abandon the problem of evil altogether, however, it is finally worth pointing out a further line of defence open to someone who thinks it possible or likely that there is a God in spite of the existence of evil. We can call it the 'Reasonableness of the Existence of God Defence' since it proceeds from the view that it is reasonable to believe in God.

As we have seen, someone who thinks that the existence of evil renders the existence of God impossible or unlikely is arguing as follows:

Evil exists.
If evil exists, it is impossible or unlikely that God exists.
Therefore, it is impossible or unlikely that God exists.

Now this argument is valid, though that is not to say that its premises and conclusion are true. But suppose one had very good reason for believing that God exists. In that case one would certainly have reason for saying that God's existence is possible. One would also have reason for denying that evil makes it unlikely that God exists since one would already have good reason to believe that God does exist. One might therefore offer the following argument:

God exists.
Evil exists.
Therefore both God and evil exist and the existence of evil does not make it impossible or unlikely that God exists.

Now there may be no good reason for believing in the existence of God. But if someone thought he had a good reason he would surely be justified in using the second of the above arguments in response to the assertion that belief in God can be dismissed in advance because of the problem of evil. Someone who wanted to reject belief in God without reference to reasons for belief in God might find such a move tiresome; but he could only show that it was unreasonable by shifting his ground. In other words, he would now have to start engaging with the believer's reasons for believing in the existence of God.

At this point in our discussion, therefore, perhaps we can join him. To begin with, we shall turn to a line of argument whose philosophical career has been long and various. It centres on the meaning of the word 'God'.

4 The ontological argument

'What's in a name?' asked Juliet. It could be said that defenders of the Ontological Argument think there can be quite a lot. Before we see why, however, I ought to point out that there is actually no single argument which alone deserves to be called 'The Ontological Argument'. For reasons of convention and convenience I retain the title as a chapter-heading. I also sometimes use the expression 'the ontological argument'. But 'the ontological argument' is best taken as referring to a group of related arguments.

Ontological arguments

The most famous form of the ontological argument is to be found in St. Anselm's *Proslogion*, Chapter 2, where we find Anselm apparently offering a definition of God. God, he says, is 'something than which nothing greater can be thought' (*aliquid quo nihil maius cogitari possit*). Anselm's question is whether God, so understood, exists; and his reply takes the form of a *reductio ad absurdum* argument – an argument whose aim is to show that a proposition is true because its denial entails a contradiction or some other absurdity.

Anselm quotes the beginning of Psalm 52: 'The fool says in his heart "There is no God".' The fool, says Anselm, at least understands what it is whose existence he is denying. Thus, says Anselm, he has the idea of God 'in his mind' (*in intellectu*). But God, he continues, must be more than an idea in someone's mind if he is also something than which nothing greater can be thought, for otherwise he would not be something than which nothing greater can be thought. It follows, says Anselm, that God must exist in reality (*in re*) as well as in the mind.

Even the Fool, then, is forced to agree that something-than-which-nothing-greater-can-be-thought exists in the mind, since he understands this when he hears it, and whatever is understood is in the mind. And surely that-than-which-a-greater-cannot-be-thought cannot exist in the mind alone. For if it exists solely in the mind even, it can be thought to exist in reality also, which is greater. If then that-than-which-a-greater-cannot-be-thought exists in the mind alone, this same that-than-which-a-greater-cannot-be-thought is that-than-which-a-greater-can-be-thought. But this is obviously impossible. Therefore there is absolutely no doubt that something-than-which-a-greater-cannot-be-thought exists both in the mind and in reality.[1]

Thus Anselm seems to be deducing the real existence of God from the concept of God, and, for this reason, his argument can be called *a priori*. In other words, it tries to reach its conclusion not by considering evidence of a tangible nature – as when one argues from a specimen that a patient has anaemia – but by considering meanings or ideas or definitions.

So much, then, for Anselm's version of the ontological argument. But the argument also has several other notable forms. In particular, there are those defended by René Descartes (1591-1650), Norman Malcolm, and Alvin Plantinga.

Descartes's argument comes in the fifth of his *Meditations*.[2] According to Descartes, just as one can have a clear and distinct idea of numbers or figures so one can have a clear and distinct idea of God. And as Descartes sees it, the idea of God is the idea of supremely perfect being. Furthermore, this being can be seen to have 'an actual and eternal existence' just as some number or figures can be seen to have some kind of character or attribute.

Existence can no more be separated from the essence of God than can its having its three angles equal to two right angles be separated from the essence of a rectilinear triangle, or the idea of a mountain from the idea of a valley; and so there is not any less repugnance to our conceiving a God (that is, a Being supremely perfect) to whom existence is lacking (that is to say, to whom a certain perfection is lacking), than to conceive of a mountain which has no valley.[3]

The idea here seems to be that from the notion of God one can deduce his existence. God is supremely perfect and must therefore exist.

Malcolm's version of the ontological argument[4] begins by trying to remove certain difficulties. Philosophers often object to the ontological argument by saying that it wrongly treats existence as a perfection which things may have or lack. Malcolm agrees with this criticism and he also allows that Anselm is subject to it. According to Malcolm, Anselm supposes that existence is a perfection in his statement of the ontological argument in *Proslogion* 2. But Malcolm also thinks that Anselm has an ontological argument that does not assume that existence is a perfection. In *Proslogion* 3 we come across the following passage:

And this being (sc. God) so truly exists that it cannot be even thought not to exist. For something can be thought to exist that cannot be thought not to exist, and this is greater than that which can be thought not to exist. Hence, if that-than-which-a-greater-cannot-be-thought can be thought not to exist, then that-than-which-a-greater-cannot-be-thought is not the same as that-than-which-a-greater-cannot-be-thought, which is absurd. Something-than-which-a-greater-cannot-be-thought exists so truly then, that it cannot be even thought not to exist.

According to Malcolm, Anselm is saying here not that God must exist because existence is a perfection, but that God must exist because the concept of God is the concept of a being whose existence is necessary. As Malcolm sees it, Anselm's *Proslogion* 3 considers God as a being who, if he exists, has the property of necessary existence. Since, however, a being who has this property cannot fail to exist it follows that God actually exists.

If God, a being a greater than which cannot be conceived, does not exist then He cannot *come* into existence. For if He did He would either have been *caused* to come into existence or have *happened* to come into existence, and in either case He would be a limited being, which by our conception of Him He is not. Since He cannot come into existence, if He does not exist His existence is impossible. If He does exist He cannot have come into existence . . . nor can He cease to exist, for nothing could cause him to cease to exist nor could it just happen that He ceased to exist. So if God exists His existence is necessary. Thus God's existence is either impossible or necessary. It can be the former only if the concept of such a being is self-contradictory or in some way logically absurd. Assuming that this is not so, it follows that He necessarily exists.[5]

This argument is criticized by Plantinga, but Plantinga argues that it can be salvaged if restated with the help of the philosophical notion of possible worlds, a notion popularized through the writings of a group commonly known as modal logicians.[6] Roughly speaking, a possible world is a way things might have been. Our world is a possible world. So too is a world exactly like ours but where, for example, elephants have two trunks instead of one. Working with this notion of possible worlds, therefore, Plantinga first formulates Malcolm's argument in two propositions:

1. There is a world, W, in which there exists a being with maximal greatness,

and

2. A being has maximal greatness in a world only if it exists in every world.[7]

According to Plantinga, this argument establishes that in some possible world there is a being with maximal greatness. And a world containing such a being contains an essence, E, which entails the property 'exists in every world'. Unfortunately, however, says Plantinga, the argument does not establish that there is a being who enjoys maximal greatness in our world. For, presumably, there would be more to being maximally great than just existing in every world, and Malcolm's argument only shows that in some world a being is maximally great.

But Plantinga thinks that the ontological argument can be defended and at this point he begins his defence. If he is right in his assessment of Malcolm's argument it follows that there is a possible world where a being has maximal greatness, which entails that the being exists in every world. But it does not entail that in every world the being is greater or more perfect than other inhabitants of those worlds. Plantinga therefore introduces the notion of maximal excellence. Maximal excellence is connected with maximal greatness.

> The property *has maximal greatness* entails the property *has maximal excellence in every possible world.*

> Maximal excellence entails *omniscience*, *omnipotence*, and *moral perfection.*[8]

Now, says Plantinga, maximal greatness is possibly exemplified. There is a possible world where there is a being who is maximally great. In that case, however, there is a world with a being who has maximal excellence, from which it follows that in any possible world there is a being who has maximal excellence, from which it follows that there is in our world a being who has maximal excellence, which is to say that there is actually a God whose existence follows from his essence and who can thus be thought to exist in reality by reasoning that counts as a form of the ontological argument.

How successful is the ontological argument?

The argument of Anselm's *Proslogion 2* has at least one point in its favour. People offer different accounts of the nature of God, but it would normally be accepted that God must be immeasurably superior to other things or to whatever is not God. Furthermore, it seems that God cannot merely happen to exist. That might be taken to imply that God's existence was somehow conditional on something, even that it was a sort of accident. It might also be taken to imply that at some future date God could cease to exist. Anselm maintains that God is something than which nothing greater can be thought, that he is necessary or ultimate in a way that nothing apart from God is. This suggestion seems reasonable in the context of an argument for God's existence. It seems fair to suggest that no argument can count as an argument for God as traditionally conceived unless it somehow allows that God is supremely great or in some way inevitable.

But is Anselm's argument cogent? After the appearence of the *Proslogion* a monk called Gaunilo replied to Anselm and virtually accused him of absurdity. According to Gaunilo, if Anselm is correct then it is not only God's existence that can be established by reasoning akin to Anselm's.

For example: they say that there is in the ocean somewhere an island which, because of the difficulty (or rather the impossibility) of finding that which does not exist, some have called the 'Lost Island'. And the story goes that it is blessed with all manner of priceless riches and delights in abundance, much more even than the Happy Isles, and, having no owner or inhabitant, it is superior everywhere in abundance of riches to all those other lands that men inhabit. Now, if anyone tell me that it is like this, I shall easily understand what is said, since nothing is difficult about it. But if he should then go on to say, as though it were a logical consequence of this: You cannot any more doubt that this island that is more excellent than all other lands truly exists somewhere in reality than you can doubt that it is in your mind; and since it is more excellent to exist not only in the mind alone but also in reality, therefore it must needs be that it exists. For if it did not exist, any other land existing in reality would be more excellent than it, and so this island, already conceived by you to be more excellent than others, will not be more excellent. If, I say, someone wishes thus to persuade me that this island really exists beyond all doubt, I should either think that he was joking, or I should find it hard to decide which of us I ought to judge the bigger fool – I, if I agreed with him, or he, if he thought that he had proved the existence of this island with any certainty, unless he had first convinced me that its very excellence exists in my mind precisely as a thing existing truly and indubitably and not just as something unreal or doubtfully real.[9]

There is one reply that Anselm could make against this objection. For Anselm never talks about something that is in fact greater than anything else. He talks about God as something than which nothing greater can be conceived. Gaunilo refers to an island which might be better than all the islands that there are. But Anselm refers to God as something that cannot be surpassed in any respect. It might thus be suggested that to some extent Anselm and Gaunilo are talking at cross-purposes.

A defender of Gaunilo might, however, accept this point and still try to preserve the thrust of his argument. What if we take it as urging that if Anselm's argument works then it is possible to establish the existence not of the island which is better than all others, but of the island than which no more perfect island can be conceived?

The move has seemed plausible to many, but it need not really show that Anselm is talking nonsense. For it depends on assuming the coherence of the concept of an island than which no island more perfect can be conceived. Yet no matter what description of an island is provided, it is always possible that something could be added to it so as to give an account of a better island. As Plantinga puts it:

No matter how great an island is, no matter how many Nubian maidens and dancing girls adorn it, there could always be a greater – one with twice as many, for example. The qualities that make for greatness in islands – number of palm trees, amount and quality of coconuts, for example – most of these qualities have no *intrinsic maximum*. That is, there is no degree of productivity or number of palm trees (or of dancing girls) such that it is impossible that an island display more of that quality. So the idea of a greatest possible island is an inconsistent or incoherent idea; it's not possible that there be such a thing.[10]

Perhaps, then, we might conclude that Anselm's position survives the attack of Gaunilo. The trouble now, however, is that there is a possible snag for Anselm in the very point which he might urge against Gaunilo. If the idea of the greatest possible island is incoherent, must not the same be true of the idea of the greatest possible being? Some of the attributes of a perfect being might be said to have an intrinsic maximum, but it is not at all clear that all of them do. Suppose, for example, it is said that a perfect being is totally loving. Might it not be replied that the idea of a perfectly loving being is incoherent if it is taken to imply that there can be a being who is loving such that nothing more loving can be imagined? The reader might like to think about this question, but perhaps I can now simply note that there is a possible difficulty here for Anselm and pass on to consider whether his argument in *Proslogion 2* is vulnerable for reasons other than those so far introduced. And at this point it is worth referring to Kant, for it is commonly claimed that Kant provided absolutely decisive objections to Anselm's argument.

The substance of Kant's objection to the ontological argument can be briefly stated thus:

1. No existential proposition is logically necessary.
2. 'Existence' is not a real predicate.

In Kant's own words, 1 is expressed thus:

If, in an identical proposition, I reject the predicate while retaining the subject, contradiction results; and I therefore say that the former belongs necessarily to the latter. But if we reject the subject and predicate alike, there is no contradiction; for nothing is then left that can be contradicted. To posit a triangle, and yet to reject its three angles, is self-contradictory; but there is no contradiction in rejecting the triangle together with its three angles. The same holds true of the concept of an absolutely necessary being. If its existence is rejected, we reject the thing itself with all its predicates; and no question of contradiction can then arise. There is nothing outside it that would be contradicted, since the necessity of the thing is not supposed to be derived from anything external; nor is there anything internal that would be contradicted, since in rejecting the thing itself we have at the same time rejected all its internal properties. . . . I cannot form the least concept of a thing which, should it be rejected with all its predicates, leaves behind a contradiction.[11]

But is this reasoning acceptable? Many writers find it impressive, but it is far from clear that they are right to do so. According to Kant, if one said 'God does not exist' then 'nothing outside' the concept of God would 'be contradicted'. But what does this mean? Kant might mean that 'God does not exist' cannot contradict 'God exists'. But 'God does not exist' and 'God exists' do seem to contradict each other. Perhaps Kant thinks that God need not exist since the notion of a necessary being would have to be contradicted by some object outside it. But, if this is Kant's argument, it is difficult to make sense of his proposal. It is normally propositions that contradict each other. People can be said to contradict each other, and they can also be said to contradict propositions; but if Kant is saying that people contradict the view that there is a necessary being then he is not saying anything of great philosophical importance. The question is whether people who contradict the view that there can be a necessary being can be right to do so. It might be replied that they can, since no existential proposition is logically necessary. But this view would be challenged by many philosophers. Thus, for example, Swinburne writes: 'Some things do exist of logical necessity. . . . There exists a number greater than one million – and it is a logically necessary truth that there does. There exist concepts which include other concepts. . . . Certain numbers and concepts and similar things (such as logical truths) have logically necessary existence.'[12]

In short, the first part of Kant's critique of the ontological argument does not seem unanswerable. Let us then proceed to Kant's second point, which is stated by him in the following passage:

'Being' is obviously not a real predicate; that is, it is not a concept of something which could be added to the concept of a thing. It is merely the positing of a thing, or of certain determinations, as existing in themselves. Logically, it is merely the copula of a judgement. . . . If, now, we take the subject (God) with all its predicates (among which is omnipotence), and say 'God is' or 'There is God', we attach no new predicate to the concept of God, but only posit the subject in itself with all its predicates, and indeed posit it as being an *object* that stands in relation to my *concept*. The content of both must be one and the same. . . . Otherwise stated, the real contains no more than the merely possible. A hundred real thalers do not contain the least coin more than a hundred possible thalers.[13]

What does Kant mean by saying that 'Being' is not a real predicate? His point seems to be that when we say that something exists we are not ascribing to it some quality, attribute, or characteristic. And, although this suggestion is sometimes challenged, it seems to me to be correct. For, surely, to say that something exists is always to say that some concept or description is exemplified or instantiated. When I say that the Tower of London exists and that the man who assassinated Hitler does not exist I am not first talking about two things and then giving you more information about what they are like. I am saying that what is contained in two respective concepts is in the one case to be found in the real world and in the other not. Gottlob Frege (1848-1925) puts this point by saying that 'existence' is a second-order predicate. When one is dealing with a first-order predicate one is dealing with a term that tells one something about the nature of something. In 'The man in the house is bald', 'bald' is a first-order predicate. In the case of a second-order predicate, however, we are dealing with a term that tells us something about a concept rather than about the nature of some object. Thus in 'Horses are numerous', 'numerous' does not tell us what horses are like, as, for example, does 'are four-legged'; so 'numerous' functions here as a second-order predicate. It tells us that the concept 'horse' is instantiated many times.

And here, perhaps, we really do have an answer to the argument of *Proslogion* 2. For Anselm's argument does appear to take existence as an attribute, quality, or characteristic. It has been suggested that Anselm does not regard existence in this way; but this supposition is hard to square with his talk about greatness. His argument seems to be that God must exist *in re* if he is that than which nothing greater can be thought. So, as Anselm sees it, to exist must be to have some kind of great-making quality. And since a great-making quality must be some kind of attribute, quality, or characteristic, it follows that Anselm regards existence as a predicate in the sense covered by Frege's notion of a first-order predicate.

The above criticism of Anselm also applies to Descartes's argument. Certainly Descartes is right to say that there is a concept of God suggesting that 'God does not exist' is nonsense. There is indeed a sense in which we can regard 'God does not exist' as absurd in the way that 'This triangle has four sides' is absurd. For how can you have a non-existent God? But this argument does not show that there actually is a God. Descartes is treating existence as a property; he explicitly says that it is a perfection. Yet existence as actuality is not a perfection, not a predicate that tells one something about the nature of something. Even in Descartes's day the thrust of this point was recognized. Pierre Gassendi (1592–1655) replied to Descartes by saying: 'Existence is a perfection neither in God nor in anything else; it is rather that in the absence of which there is no perfection . . . in enumerating the perfections of God, you ought not to have put existence among them, in order to draw the conclusion that God exists, unless you wanted to beg the question.'[14]

I suggest, then, that, because of their attempt to treat 'exists' as a first-order predicate, the argument of *Proslogion* 2 and the argument of Descartes are difficult to accept. This is not to say that 'exists' can *never* be used as a predicate.[15] But Anselm and Descartes seem to hold that something is a member of the real world, where 'being a member of the real world' is some kind of property that things can have or lack. And this suggestion is misguided.

Thus we come to the version of the ontological argument defended by

Malcolm and Plantinga. It might be worth noting in advance that Malcolm is arguably wrong to read *Proslogion* 3 as a separate attempt to show that there is a God. It has, for instance, been plausibly maintained that *Proslogion* 3 is trying to show that something is true of the actual God, not that there is an actual God. But this exegetical point need not detain us. Malcolm's argument may not be Anselm's, but it is still an argument and we can ask if it is cogent.

The first thing to be said is that Malcolm has made a valid enough distinction in his account of existence and necessity. He holds that we can talk of necessary existence as a property, which seems true. Something like such talk was used in medieval discussions about necessary beings. According to many medieval thinkers there are beings which, as a matter of fact, could not be generated or made to corrupt. If, then, we use the word 'necessary' in the medieval sense meant in the expression 'necessary being' it is easy to see how necessary existence can be thought of as a property. A being will have necessary existence if it is a necessary being in the medieval sense, and since such beings were understood with reference to their inability to be generated or made to corrupt it seems that they were understood with reference to a very definite property or characteristic.

But having granted this point we can yet, I think, see that Malcolm's argument fails. One reason for saying so can be seen if we concentrate on its use of the term 'impossible'.

Remember that according to Malcolm: (1) since God cannot come into existence his existence is impossible if he does not exist; (2) if God does exist, his existence is necessary; (3) God's existence is either impossible or necessary. But 'impossible' here is being used in two senses. First it is being used to mean 'as a matter of fact unable to come about', for when Malcolm first talks about impossibility he is expressing the view that if God is in fact the sort of thing that cannot come into existence then if God does not exist he cannot in fact exist at all, for his existing depends on his not being brought into existence. In the second sense, however, 'impossible' is being used to mean 'unable to be thought without contradition', for Malcolm explains that if God's existence is impossible, 'the concept of such a being is self-contradictory or in some way logically absurd.' Now Malcolm's conclusion is that God's existence is necessary, i.e. the opposite of impossible. But as Malcolm presents this conclusion it must mean that the concept of God is the concept of something that is logically necessary. Thus, from 'God's non-existence is as a matter of fact impossible' Malcolm reaches the conclusion 'God's existence is logically necessary.' But that means that Malcolm is offering a very poor argument indeed. For the conclusion is presupposed by the very thing on which it is based, i.e. that there is a God whose non-existence is as a matter of fact impossible.

This point is well brought out by John Hick who, following Malcolm, distinguishes between something that cannot in fact be brought into existence and something whose non-existence is strictly inconceivable. The first kind of being Hick calls an 'ontologically necessary being'; the second he refers to as a 'logically necessary being'. Then he explains that:

Whether there is an ontologically necessary being . . . is a question of fact, although of uniquely ultimate fact. Given this concept of an ontologically necessary being, it is a matter of logic that if there is such a being, his existence is necessary in the sense that he cannot cease to exist, and that if there is no such being, none can come to exist. This logical necessity and this logical impossibility are, however, dependent upon the hypotheses, respectively, that there is and that there is not an ontologically necessary being; apart from the hypotheses from which they follow they do not entail that there is or that there is not an eternal self-existent being. Hence, there is no substance to the dilemma: The existence of God is either logically necessary or logically absurd.[17]

Another way of seeing why Malcolm's argument will not do is to begin by considering the following argument:

A pixie is a little man with pointed ears.
Therefore there actually exists a pixie.

Now clearly we would not accept this as an argument for pixies. Why not? Because it seems to move from a definition of 'pixie' to the conclusion that there actually is a pixie. But suppose someone were to reply that if a pixie *is* a little man with pointed ears then he must *be* in some sense or he would not be there to have pointed ears. That too would be an unjustifiable (if unforgettable) argument. But why? Because it fails to acknowledge that 'is' can be used in at least two different ways. 'Is' can be used in giving a definition – as in 'A novel is a work of fiction.' Or it can be used to explain that there actually is something or other – as in 'There is an abominable snowman after all.' In the first use we are not really saying anything about something that exists: 'A novel is a work of fiction' does not, for example, say anything about any existent novel. It explains what the word 'novel' means. In the second use too there is a sense in which we are not saying anything about some existent thing. But nor are we explaining what something (which may or may not exist) is. In 'There is an abominable snowman after all' we are not describing anything; nor are we explaining what we should have found if we discovered it. We are saying that an abominable snowman is what something is, and in doing so we tacitly suppose that what we are talking about actually exists. In the above argument from 'A pixie is . . .' to 'There is a pixie . . .' the arguer would be moving from a premise containing the first sense of 'is' to a conclusion containing the second. Or, as some philosophers would put it, he would be moving from an 'is' of *definition* to an 'is' of *affirmative predication*. And his argument is unacceptable just because this cannot validly be done. If it could, we could define anything we like into existence.

Returning now to Malcolm, we can see at this point that he is arguing in the same way as the person whose argument about pixies was just discussed. He is saying that if God is (definitionally) necessarily existent, then there is something which can truly be said to be necessarily existent. And here lies Malcolm's error. We can certainly agree that if God is defined as a necessary being, then God is by definition a necessary being. And if we can get people to accept our definition, we can easily convict them of self-contradiction if they also say that God is not a necessary being. For then they would be saying both that God is and that he is not by definition a necessary being. But we cannot move from this conclusion to the conclusion that our definition of God as a necessary being entails that there is anything that actually corresponds to our definition of him as necessary. In other words, we cannot infer from 'God is a necessary being' that 'is God' is affirmatively predicable of anything. It might seem that in that case we would have to end up saying 'The necessary being does not exist', which might be thought to involve the same mistake as that involved in saying 'My mother is not my mother.' But to deny Malcolm's conclusion all we have to say is 'Possibly nothing at all is a necessary being', which is certainly not self-contradictory and may even be true.

So Malcolm's version of the ontological argument is unsuccessful. But what of Plantinga's? His argument can be briefly stated thus:

1. There is a possible world containing a being with maximal greatness.
2. Any being with maximal greatness has the property of maximal excellence in every possible world.
3. Maximal excellence entails omniscience, omnipotence, and moral perfection.
4. There is therefore a possible world where there is a being who has maximal excellence.
5. If there is a possible world where a being has maximal excellence then that being has maximal excellence in every possible world.
6. This is a possible world.
7. Therefore God exists.

Some philosophers would challenge this argument by attacking the whole notion of possible worlds, but the intricacies of this debate cannot be entered into here. Let us instead concentrate on Plantinga's interpretation of 4. As Plantinga sees it, from the fact that it is possible for there to be something having the property of maximal excellence in every world it follows that there is actually a being with maximal excellence in our world. But is this inference correct?

Let us agree that our world is a possible world. Let us also agree that a being with maximal excellence is possible and that it is therefore possible that such a being exists in every possible world. But it does not follow that there is actually any being with maximal excellence. What follows is that maximal excellence is possible. But what is merely possible does not have any real existence – not at least in the sense in which God is normally thought to have existence. And a God who exists in all possible worlds does not have any real existence either. To show the existence of God it seems that one needs more than the possibility of God. From the fact that God is possible it follows only that he is possible; not that he is actual. And, for this reason, Plantinga's argument also seems to fail.

It might be worth adding that there is a further difficulty for someone disposed to accept Plantinga's version of the ontological argument. According to Plantinga, maximal excellence entails omniscience, omnipotence, and moral perfection. Thus Plantinga's argument is one for the existence of a being who is omniscient, omnipotent, and morally perfect. But is it not possible that the notion of such a being is incoherent, i.e. that it is impossible that there should be such a being? A critic, even one who believes in an omniscient, omnipotent, morally perfect God, might well argue that it is indeed possible that the notion of such a God is incoherent. Thus it might be urged that it is possible that the God Plantinga argues for is possibly impossible, in which case it would seem that even if maximal excellence is possibly exemplified, it is also possible that it is not, that it could not be, and that Plantinga's argument based on 4 above may therefore be regarded as undemonstrable.

Conclusion

Whole books have been written on the ontological argument and, like any major philosophical argument, it is not to be lightly dismissed. But it does seem unsuccessful – at least in the forms considered here. Why is this so? Basically because definitions can take one only so far; because we can say what we mean by something without its having to be true that what we are talking about really exists. Maybe a successful ontological argument for God's existence will one day be forthcoming; but that remains to be seen.

But this is not to say that belief in God's existence is unreasonable. There may be no good ontological argument for the existence of God, but this does not mean that a good *non*-ontological argument is impossible. And, as we shall see in the next chapter, it has been maintained that there actually is such an argument.

5 The cosmological argument

We often say that something must exist because something that is so could not be so without it. A doctor, for example, may finally conclude that a patient has cancer because he is displaying certain symptoms. There are the symptoms, so there is the cancer. I now want to turn to a similar argument for the existence of God, commonly called the Cosmological Argument. This has a long history and versions of it can be found in the work of many philosophical and religious writers from the early Greek period to the present time. For many people who believe in God it is the most appealing argument of all.

Aquinas and the cosmological argument

Perhaps the most famous version of the cosmological argument is to be found in the first three of the so-called Five Ways offered by Thomas Aquinas in the first part of his *Summa Theologiae*.[1] These are sometimes even referred to as if they constituted the only real form of the cosmological argument. But what are they all about?

The key term in the First Way is 'change' or, in the Latin of Aquinas, *motus*. The word *motus* is sometimes translated 'movement' or 'motion'; but 'change' is perhaps the best English equivalent. For, as Aquinas sees it, *motus* covers what we should normally call change of quality, change of quantity, and change of place.[2]

According to Aquinas, some things are in process of change, nothing changes itself in every respect, and whatever causes something to change must itself be operative – or, as Aquinas puts it, must be *aliquid ens actu*. Aquinas also thinks that there cannot be an endless series of things causing change to take place. So the fact that things undergo change, he says, means that there is a cause of change which is not itself caused to change by anything. And this, he concludes, is what people mean by 'God'. In reaching this conclusion, however, Aquinas is not arguing chronologically. He is not saying that there cannot be an infinite series of causes of change each preceding the other in time. He does not mean that since there is now a process of change going on, there must have been an unchanged changer at some time in the *past*. As Aquinas understands it, the fact that things undergo change means that it must now be true that there is an unchanged changer.

The Second Way turns on the notions of causation and existence. 'We never observe, nor ever could,' says Aquinas, 'something causing itself, for this would mean that it preceded itself, and this is not possible.' According to the Second Way, then, the *mere existence* of something requires a cause. And in that case, says Aquinas, the existence of everything requires a cause that is not itself caused to exist by anything other than itself. Why? Because if there is no such cause, then nothing could exist at all, while, obviously, some things do exist.

Now if you eliminate a cause you also eliminate its effects, so that you cannot have a last cause nor an intermediate one, unless you have a first. Given therefore no stop in the series of causes, and hence no first cause, there would be no intermediate causes either, and no last effect, and this would be an open mistake. One is therefore forced to suppose some first cause, to which everyone gives the name 'God'.

As is the case with the First Way, this argument is not a chronological one. According to the Second Way, God exists because the present existence of things depends on the present existence of an uncaused cause.

The Third Way includes this suggestion, but it begins differently from the Second Way. According to the Third Way, some things come into existence and pass out of it. Some things, in other words, are generated and corruptible. In Aquinas's view, however, if everything were like this, then there would now have come a time when nothing existed at all. Since such a time has obviously not arrived, not all things are generated and corruptible. Some are therefore ungenerated and incorruptible, or, in Aquinas's terminology, they are necessary beings. As Aquinas sees it, however, necessary beings pose a problem. Something may be necessary, but it still exists. So what account are we to give of its existence? According to Aquinas, we cannot accept the existence of all necessary things as a kind of brute fact. There has to be something which is both necessary and not caused to exist by anything. 'But just as we must stop somewhere in a series of causes,' says Aquinas, 'so also in the series of things which must be and owe this to other things. One is forced therefore to suppose something which must be, and owes this to no other thing than itself; indeed it itself is the cause that other things must be.'

The cosmological argument in Leibniz

Since the time of Aquinas a number of philosophers have produced versions of the cosmological argument. Examples include Descartes[3] and

Samuel Clarke (1675–1729).[4] But a particularly concise version was offered by the German philosopher Gottfried Wilhelm von Leibniz
(1646–1716).

According to Leibniz, there must be a reason why things exist since
there must be a reason why anything happens at all and a reason why one
thing exists rather than another. Leibniz also holds that when one of two
possibilities is realized, then something causes this to happen. Since the
possibility of things existing has been realized over and against the
possibility of nothing existing at all, says Leibniz, there is a cause of the
existence of things, a cause which does not depend for its existence on
anything outside itself.

There is a reason in Nature why something should exist rather than nothing. This
is a consequence of the great principle that nothing happens without a reason, and
also that there must be a reason why this thing exists rather than another.

This reason must be in some real entity or cause. For a *cause* is simply a real
reason, and truths about possibilities and *necessities* . . . would not produce anything
unless those possibilities were founded on a thing which actually exists.

This entity must be necessary; otherwise a cause must be sought outside it for the
fact that it exists rather than does not exist, which is contrary to the hypothesis. This
entity is the ultimate reason for things, and is usually called by the one word 'God'.

There is, therefore, a cause for the prevalence of existence over non-existence;
or, the *necessary being is existence-creating*.[5]

Some objections to the cosmological argument

Various criticisms have been made of the cosmological argument. Let us
for the moment note some of them without comment.

The first concerns Aquinas's principle that nothing changes or moves
itself. This principle has been attacked for various reasons. It has been said
that we can easily point to things that do change or move themselves; that
we can point, for instance, to people and to animals. It has also been said
that Aquinas's principle conflicts with Newton's first law of motion. According to Anthony Kenny, this law 'wrecks the argument of the First
Way. For at any given time the rectilinear uniform motion of a body can
be explained by the principle of inertia in terms of the body's own previous
motion without appeal to any other agent.'[6]

Kenny also offers another criticism of Aquinas's First Way. The Way,
says Kenny, depends on the false assumption that something can be made
to be actually F only through the agency of something actually F. But, says
Kenny, 'A kingmaker need not himself be king, and it is not dead men who
commit murders.'[7] 'The falsifications of the principle', Kenny adds, 'are
fatal to the argument [sc. of the First Way]. For unless the principle is
true, the conclusion contradicting the possibility of a self-mover does not

follow. If something can be made F by an agent which is merely potentially F, there seems no reason why something should not actualize its own potentiality to F-ness.'[8]

Kenny also advances what he regards as a decisive refutation of the Second Way. Aquinas accepted certain theories in medieval astrology, and, in his view, things like the generation of people involve the causal activity of the sun. Kenny concentrates on these facts and suggests that they can be used to criticize the Second Way. As he puts 't himself: 'Aquinas believed that the sun was very much more than a necessary condition of human generation. The human father, he explains . . . in generation is a tool of the sun. . . . The series of causes from which the Second Way starts is a series whose existence is vouched for only by medieval astrology. . . . The First Way starts from an indisputable fact about the world; the Second starts from an archaic fiction.'[9]

Another reason offered for rejecting the cosmological argument brings us to what is sometimes called 'the problem of infinite regress'. The cosmological argument seems to be saying that there cannot be an infinite series of causes; that the buck, so to speak, stops somewhere. Aquinas, for example, says that there cannot be an infinite series of changed changers, caused causes, or necessary beings each of which owes its necessity to something else. But in reply to such points people have asked why there cannot be an infinite series of causes. They have also asked how the cosmological argument can avoid contradicting itself. If, for example, nothing causes itself, how can there be a first cause which does not itself require a cause other than itself?

It has also been maintained that there is simply no need to talk about the existence of things in the manner of writers like Aquinas and Leibniz. Both seem to be saying that we can ask why something exists when it need not and that the answer to the question is God. According to some people, however, the existence of things must just be accepted as a brute fact. In a famous radio debate with Fredrick Copleston (b. 1907), Bertrand Russell (1872–1970) was asked whether he would agree that the universe is 'gratuitous'. The reply was, 'I should say that the universe is just there, and that's all.'[10] Following a similar line of thought, John Hick writes: 'How do we know that the universe is not "a mere unintelligible brute fact"? Apart from the emotional colouring suggested by the phrase, this is precisely what the sceptic believes it to be; and to exclude this possibility at the outset is merely to beg the question at issue.'[11]

Other criticisms of the cosmological argument focus on the first part of the Third Way. First, it has been said that even if something is corruptible, it does not follow that it will actually corrupt. My cat is kickable, but does that mean that I have to kick it? Second, it has been urged that, even if we agree that everything corrupts at some time, there is no reason to think that there is some one time when everything has corrupted. Objectors to Aquinas who make this point sometimes express themselves by saying that in the Third Way Aquinas is guilty of the 'Quantifier-shift Fallacy' – the mistake which someone would be making if he thought that 'Everyone loves something' means that there is some one thing (e.g. sex) that everyone loves.[12] It has also been said that the quantifier-shift fallacy occurs in the First and Second Ways. In the First Way, so the argument goes, Aquinas erroneously moves from 'Everything is changed by something' to 'Some one thing changes everything.' In the Second Way, Aquinas mistakenly infers 'There is one efficient cause of everything' from 'Everything has an efficient cause.' In this connection the reader might care to note a remark made by Russell in the above-mentioned debate with Copleston. According to Copleston, the existence of the universe must be caused. Russell replies: 'I can illustrate what seems to me your fallacy. Every man who exists has a mother, and it seems to me that your argument is that therefore the human race must have a mother, but obviously the human race hasn't a mother – that's a different logical sphere.'[13]

Is the cosmological argument reasonable?

We have now noted some classic formulations of the cosmological argument; we have also noted some criticisms that have been made of them. Now we need to ask whether the argument is a reasonable one.

Perhaps the first thing to say is that some of the criticisms levelled against it are either unfair or inconclusive. Take, for example, Kenny's claim that the Second Way can be rejected because it depends on theories in medieval astrology. This claim is not very plausible. A supporter of Aquinas may well allow that Aquinas held odd views about astrology. He may therefore concede that many particular causal explanations which Aquinas might give of particular events are demonstrably mistaken. But he can also add that this point is utterly irrelevant to the argument of the Second Way. As the text of the Way seems to suggest, the Second Way is concerned with general causal questions rather than particular ones. In a sense it is arguing about causality itself.

It might be replied that, even if we accept this point, there remains Kenny's argument that something not actually F can make something potentially F become actually F. But this argument too can be criticized. It is clearly true, as Kenny suggests, that kingmakers need not be kings and that dead men do not commit murders. But the First Way does not subscribe to the principle that only what is actually F will make something potentially F actually F. And it would be odd if it did. Apart from the fact that Kenny's counter-examples are so obvious that one could reasonably expect a thinker of Aquinas's stature to have anticipated them, the principle conflicts with medieval views about the temperature of the sun which Aquinas endorses in commentary on the Greek philosopher Aristotle (384–322 BC).[14] Furthermore, if Aquinas maintained that only what was actually F could make things become F he would be committed to saying that, for instance, God is hot, cold, pink, and fluffy. For Aquinas holds that God accounts for the changes that occur in the world. But Aquinas would clearly not want to talk of God being hot, cold, pink, or fluffy. For a start, he would say that God is not a body.[15] As is clear from the text of the First Way, what Aquinas wants to say is that only something *real* will bring about a change to being F in something that is potentially F. The First Way also seems to imply that only something with the power to make something F can ultimately account for something becoming F. But this view is evidently not affected by Kenny's examples. A kingmaker need not be a king, but he must have the power to make kings. A murderer cannot be a corpse, but he must have the power to kill.

But these points do not show that the cosmological argument is acceptable. Suppose then we proceed to what can fairly be regarded as its heart. This comprises two suggestions: (1) that there is a cause of the existence of things, and (2) that this cause does not itself require a cause of its existence outside itself.

Is it reasonable to accept (1)? As we have seen, a writer like Russell would say that there is no need to accept it at all. He holds that the existence of things can reasonably be regarded as a brute fact. But is this view reasonable?

It would be if one could accept a view of causation often associated with David Hume. He argues that it is possible to conceive of an effect without conceiving of the cause of that effect, and he concludes that given any supposed effect E which is normally said to be caused by C, we can yet affirm E without implying that C ever existed at all. 'When we look about us towards external objects, and consider the operation of causes, we are never able, in a single instance, to discover any power or necessary connection; any quality, which binds the effect to the cause, and renders the one an infallible consequence of the other.'[16]

But if this view of causation is offered in defence of the view that there is no cause of the existence of things, it is open to a rejoinder. For we normally do agree that we have to ask what brings it about that particular things exist. And this point is important in considering the cosmological argument.

It would help to reflect for a moment on an important part of our intellectual activity – our tendency to ask how it is that something is the case when it need not have been. We display this tendency continually, and to do so is part of what it is to be human. We get up in the morning and we find a puddle on the landing, so we ask how the puddle has come to be there. This sort of questioning goes on all through our lives: the presence of things that do not have to be there naturally sets us thinking.

Now it is important to see that there are different sorts of answers that can be appropriate when we ask why something is the case. I may ask why the puddle is there on the landing and at one level this question might be satisfactorily answered by the reply that the water-tank has sprung a leak. That is a crude kind of explanation perhaps, but it is perfectly in order and it tries to state what past events led up to some present state of affairs. But another kind of answer might be possible, and in a sense it would be more comprehensive. One may try to account for the puddle in terms belonging to what we normally think of as science; by referring, that is, to the physical laws in the universe that make puddles possible – the physics and chemistry of puddles. Finally, however, my question about the puddle can go even deeper. Here is a puddle; a puddle exists. How come the *sheer existence* of the puddle? This is not a scientific question. There may be scientific laws which explain how I can end up with a puddle on my landing on some particular day; but these laws will not explain why there is a puddle rather than nothing at all. For the question now raised can be applied to whatever obeys scientific laws. It broadens out, in fact, to a much more difficult question, the question of why there is something rather than nothing. There might, after all, have been nothing at all. So how does it come about that there is anything?

As we have seen, some would say that this question ought not to be asked, that the mere existence of things does not raise the question 'How come?' But this view is an extremely odd one. Confronted by human beings when there might have been only apes or fish, we ask 'How come?' Confronted by a puddle when there might have been a dry landing, we ask 'How come?' And confronted by something when there might have been nothing at all, we ought surely to ask again 'How come?'

One might reply that this view is unreasonable; and if the reader chooses to do so, there are many philosophers who would agree with him. Yet it must also be said, I think, that the reply is a difficult one to accept. Even Hume seems to have felt this, in spite of what he argues about cause and effect. In a letter written in 1754 he says: 'But allow me to tell you that I never asserted so absurd a Proposition as *that anything might arise without a cause*: I only maintain'd that, our Certainty of the Falsehood of that Proposition proceeded neither from Intuition nor Demonstration; but from another Source.'[17] In a similar vein C. D. Broad (1887–1971) explains that 'whatever I may *say* when I am trying to give Hume a run for his money, I cannot really *believe in* anything beginning to exist without being *caused* (in the old-fashioned sense of *produced* or *generated*) by something else which existed before and up to the moment when the entity in question began to exist.'[18]

One way of disregarding such a view would be to appeal again to Hume's argument about the possibility of disuniting cause and effect. But is Hume's argument such as to make it reasonable to disbelieve in the intuitive correctness of the view that if X exists then X is caused to exist by something else? As Elizabeth Anscombe indicates, it is not such at all. Hume writes:

. . . as all distinct ideas are separable from each other, and as the ideas of cause and effect are evidently distinct, 'twill be easy for us to conceive any object to be non-existent this moment, and existent the next, without conjoining to it the distinct idea of a cause or productive principle. The separation, therefore, of the idea of a cause from that of a beginning of existence, is plainly possible for the imagination; and consequently the actual separation of these objects is so far possible, that it implies no contradiction or absurdity; and is therefore incapable of being refuted by any reasoning from mere ideas; without which 'tis impossible to demonstrate the necessity of a cause.[19]

But this argument only asserts that because we can imagine something coming into existence without a cause it is possible that something really can come into existence without a cause. And, as Anscombe observes of this assertion:

The trouble about it is that it is very unconvincing. For if I say I can imagine a rabbit coming into being without a parent rabbit, well and good: I imagine a rabbit coming into being, and our observing that there is no parent rabbit about. But what am I to imagine if I imagine a rabbit coming into being without a cause? Well, I just imagine a rabbit coming into being. That this *is* the imagination of a rabbit coming into being without a cause is nothing but, as it were, the *title* of the picture. Indeed I can form an image and give my picture that title. But from my being able to do *that*, nothing whatever follows about what it is possible to suppose 'without contradiction or absurdity' as holding in reality.[20]

The reader may care to ponder things further for himself at this stage, but at present I suggest that the existence of things does raise a question about a cause of their existence. And thus I suggest that the first major stage of the cosmological argument is reasonable. But what of the second stage? Why say that the cause of existing things does not require a cause of its existence? If it is reasonable to assert that there is a cause of the existence of things, is it not reasonable to ask 'What causes the existence of the cause of existing things?' For must not the cause of existing things exist?

At this point in the discussion we evidently find ourselves confronted with the criticism of the cosmological argument based on the possibility of an infinite regress. If it is true of A that it is caused to exist by B, why may not B be caused to exist by C, D, E . . . and so on *ad infinitum?* But this question does not have to embarrass someone who wishes to defend the cosmological argument. For if it is said of all existing things that there is a question about what brings them into existence, it does not follow that the question 'What brings it into existence?' is a legitimate question to ask about what brings existing things into existence. For if there actually is a cause of all existing things, but if that cause requires a cause and that cause another and so on *ad infinitum,* then nothing will exist at all. If it is true that the mere existence of things requires a cause, but if there is no first cause of which this cannot be said, then all the things which exist will only be caused by what shares with them the need to be accounted for with reference to a cause. Or, in other words, there will be nothing but effects, which cannot be since if something is an effect it must be caused. That follows from the meaning of the word 'effect'.

But at this point there is another difficulty to mention. Someone might ask, 'If all existing things require a cause, how can there be a first cause which does not itself require a cause?' Suppose now we concentrate on the use of the word 'thing' in this question. Might it not be urged that the cosmological argument is self-contradictory since it *asserts* of all *things* that they require a cause but *denies* of one *thing* that it requires a cause?

If the cosmological argument does work like this, then it would indeed seem that the argument contains some kind of contradiction. But if we look back now to something that I argued in Chapter 3, we can see that the contradiction need only be regarded as apparent. In Chapter 3 I argued that if we are talking about God, and if we regard God as the source of existing things, then we could say that God is not a being. Another way of making this point is to deny that the cause of existing things is in a genus or is a genus. It could therefore be said that the cosmological argument can work on the assumption that the cause of existing things is not a thing, in which case the above contradiction would disappear.

In talking about the cause of existing things, then, the cosmological argument could be regarded as talking about what is radically different from any particular thing. But does not this fact raise even more problems for the defender of the cosmological argument? Can he say that when he talks about the cause of existing things he can think of this (*a*) as not an existing thing, i.e. as something that is not locatable generically, and (*b*) as a cause?

It seems to me that an affirmative answer is possible here. For the term 'cause' is not a generic one. To learn that something is a cause is not to learn what it is in itself. Thus, if a doctor says that something must be causing the patient's symptoms, he is not committed to saying that he knows what the cause is. So if someone says that there is a cause of existing things, he is not committed to holding that it is itself some kind of existing thing. On the other hand, he may, as I have suggested, have reason to say that there is a cause of existing things. And this by itself will give him reason to deny that this cause is an existing thing that requires (by virtue of that fact) a distinct cause of its existence. For, as I have suggested, if X is the cause of all existing things, then X is not a particular thing. And if X is the cause of all existing things, then X is not itself like what it causes in the sense that it is not such as to provoke the question 'What cause brings about its existence?'

The cosmological argument and God

It seems, then, that the kernel of the cosmological argument is reasonable. Only it turns out that in talking of a cause of existing things we are talking about a cause that is not an existing thing and which is better spoken of as if it were not either in a genus or itself a genus. But does this mean that the cosmological argument is a reasonable argument for God?

Here we come to a problem that is best introduced by some famous remarks of Hume. In his *Enquiry concerning Human Understanding* he writes:

When we infer any particular cause from an effect, we must proportion the one to the other, and can never be allowed to ascribe to the cause any qualities, but what are exactly sufficient to produce the effect. . . . If the cause assigned for any effect, be not sufficient to produce it, we must either reject that cause, or add to it such qualities as will give it a just proportion to the effect. But if we ascribe to it farther qualities, or affirm it capable of producing other effects, we can only indulge the licence of conjecture, and arbitrarily suppose the existence of qualities and energies without reason or authority.[21]

Now it seems reasonable to say that when people talk of God they suppose themselves to be talking of something of which various things can be said. Remember Owen's definition of classical theism according to which God is one, perfect, omniscient, omnipotent, and eternal. As I have discussed it, the cosmological argument seems to give reason for talking about a cause of all existing things, but can one identify this cause with God as referred to, for example, in classical theism? Can one not take Hume's point and urge that, in regarding the cosmological argument as an argument for God, one is inferring beyond known effects and ascribing more qualities than are exactly sufficient to produce them?

The meaning of the terms which believers use in talking about God is a matter of considerable debate among both philosophers and theologians. But even without going into their meaning in detail one can, I think, say something about the legitimacy of applying them to the cause to which the cosmological argument concludes. Here, five main points can be made.

(1) 'X is caused to exist' leaves open the possibility of X being caused to exist by more than one thing. And, obviously, when we say that something is caused to exist we do not always mean that one thing causes it to exist. Thus we can hold that the existence of the child is caused by both its parents. But if the cosmological argument is cogent, it would be reasonable to say that there could not be many Gods. For to say that there could be many Xs presupposes that X can introduce a unit of counting, i.e. it presupposes that the term 'X' can be used to refer to things that can be counted. But if something cannot be regarded as belonging to a genus or as being a genus then it cannot be counted, since one cannot mark it off and number its instances by contrast to other things. That is why a term like 'cause' does not by itself refer to something that can be counted. One would only be able to count causes if one knew what kind of causes one was expected to count.[22]

If all this is true, however, the cosmological argument does not really justify one in talking about one God. But those who say that there is one God are usually only trying to rule out the suggestion that there are many causes of the existence of all things, i.e. they are preferring the language of monotheism to that of polytheism. If, then, 'God is one' simply means that one cannot regard the existence of all things as a reason for accepting that there are many causes of the existence of all things, then it can be said that the cosmological argument gives one grounds for saying that God is one, assuming that one wishes to identify God with the cause of all existing things. For, as we have seen, it is not possible to count whatever is said to be the cause of the existence of all things.

(2) To say that something is perfect is to say that it is as good as it can be given the kind of thing it is. The term 'perfect' is relative in the sense that if X is truly said to be perfect it does not follow that the grounds for calling X perfect will justify us in calling Y perfect. A perfect circle is not perfect for the same reason as a perfect typewriter. So to say that God is perfect cannot be to say that God possesses all possible perfections as these are possessed by whatever possesses them. It cannot, for example, be to say that God is perfectly sound-proof since God is usually said to be incorporeal and since it makes no sense to apply 'sound-proof' to what is incorporeal. To say that God is perfect must therefore be to say that God does not lack any perfection appropriate to God. But it is usually said that omniscience is a perfection appropriate to God. As we shall see in a moment, however (under (3)), the cosmological argument does not give reason for holding that the cause of all existing things is omniscient. Therefore it does not give reason for holding that the cause of all existing things is perfect as God is said to be perfect.

(3) Whatever might be the full meaning of 'omniscient' it is clear that anything said to be omniscient must be very knowledgeable. Yet just because X is able to cause something to come into existence it does not follow that X is even conscious, let alone omniscient. For 'cause', as we have seen, is not a generic term. So on the basis of the cosmological argument alone there is no reason to conclude that the cause of all existing things is omniscient.

(4) Whatever might be the full meaning of 'omnipotent' it is clear that anything said to be omnipotent must be very powerful. Now if everything that exists is caused to exist by X then X must be very powerful since it is able to bring all things into existence. If X is said to bring all things into existence, but if X is also said not to be 'very powerful', then 'very powerful' is being used in a very odd sense indeed.

(5) 'Eternal' (as we shall see in Chapter 8) has been applied to God in two ways. According to the first, to say that God is eternal is to say that he is timeless. According to the second, it is to say that he will exist for ever. Many philosophers would argue that something can only be said to be in time if it exists as part of a world of changing things. If this view is correct it follows that the cause to which the cosmological argument concludes must be eternal *qua* timeless since it is the cause of all things and since the class of all things clearly includes the class of changing things. But if 'eternal' means 'of endless duration' it does not follow that the cause to which the cosmological argument concludes is eternal. For the argument does not show that this cause cannot cease to exist. It merely shows that it exists if particular things exist and that its existence is not caused by any particular cause outside itself.

The position, then, appears to be rather complicated. As an argument for a first cause of all existing things the cosmological argument seems a reasonable one. But it does not by itself establish the existence of God with all the properties sometimes ascribed to him. Many people who believe in God would, however, say that this does not matter. They would argue that apart from the cosmological argument there is reason to believe in God and that when this reason is put together with the cosmological argument one is left with a rational case for belief in God together with the properties that are usually ascribed to him. But at this stage in our discussion this view cannot be assessed at all. Before anything can be said on the matter it is necessary to consider other reasons that have been offered for belief in God.

6 The argument from design

People concerned to offer grounds for belief in God have often resorted to the Argument from Design, sometimes called the 'Teleological Argument'; and it is to this argument that I now want to turn. Like the ontological and cosmological arguments, however, the argument from design comes in different forms. To begin with, therefore, I shall say something about these forms.

Versions of the argument from design

One of the earliest statements of the argument from design comes in Cicero's *De Natura Deorum*.[1] Here, a figure called Lucilius asks: 'What could be more clear or obvious when we look up to the sky and contemplate the heavens, than that there is some divinity of superior intelligence?' The point Lucilius seems to be making here is that the operation of the universe must be somehow controlled by intelligence; and this idea is at the heart of all versions of the argument from design.

But what is it about the operation of the universe that convinces people that the universe bears the mark of divine intelligence? Here we need to distinguish two different notions of design.

First, there is design *qua* regularity. Instances of this would be a succession of regular marks on paper, a musical score, or the arrangement of flowers in a garden at Versailles. On the other hand, there is design *qua* purpose. We should be working with this sense of 'design' if we talked about something being designed because it had parts put together for some end or other, as in the case of a radio or television set. With this distinction in mind, we can now note two lines of argument offered by people who claim to see in the universe evidence of design: the first states that the universe displays design *qua* regularity and the second that it displays design *qua* purpose.

One version of an argument from design *qua* regularity is defended by Richard Swinburne. He writes:

Almost all objects in the world behave in a highly regular way describable by scientific laws. . . . The most general regularities of all are, as such, scientifically inexplicable. The question arises whether there is a possible explanation of another kind which can be provided for them, and whether their occurrence gives any or much support to that explanation. . . . Since actions of agents can explain regularities . . . the action of an agent could explain the regular behaviour of the matter of the universe, the behaviour codified in scientific laws. All the regularity in nature would be due to the action of a postulated god, making nature, as it were, perform a great symphony in the way in which a man produces from his throat a regular series of notes.[2]

Perhaps the most famous form of an argument from design *qua* purpose is that defended by William Paley (1743–1805) in his book *Natural Theology*.[3] 'In crossing a heath,' says Paley,

suppose I pitched my foot against a *stone*, and were asked how the stone came to be there: I might possibly answer, that, for anything I knew to the contrary, it had lain there for ever; nor would it, perhaps, be very easy to show the absurdity of this answer. But suppose I found a *watch* upon the ground, and it should be inquired how the watch happened to be in that place. I should hardly think of the answer I had before given – that, for anything I knew, the watch might always have been there. Yet why should not this answer serve for the watch as well as for the stone?[4]

Paley's reply is that the parts of the watch are obviously put together to achieve a definite result: 'When we come to inspect the watch, we perceive (what we could not discover in the stone) that its several parts are framed and put together for a purpose, e.g. that they are so formed and adjusted as to produce motion, and that motion so regulated as to point out the hour of the day. . . .'[5] Paley's suggestion now is that the universe resembles the watch and must therefore be accounted for in terms of intelligent and purposive agency:

Every indication of contrivance, every manifestation of design, which existed in the watch, exists in the works of nature; with the difference, on the side of nature, of being greater and more, and that in a degree which exceeds all computation. I mean, that the contrivances of nature surpass the contrivances of art, in the complexity, subtilty, and curiosity of the mechanism.[6]

Kant and the argument from design

It has often been argued that a fairly decisive refutation of the argument from design is available if we take to heart some arguments of Kant. All forms of the argument seem to suppose that there really is in the universe some kind of order which is independent of our minds, something we come across rather than manufacture for ourselves. As Kant sees it, how-

ever, we would impose order on whatever universe we were in, for only so
could we think and reason as we do. According to Kant, we are unable to
experience 'things in themselves'; we are presented in experience with an
undifferentiated manifold and we order our experience of things in themselves as our understanding imposes such categories as unity and plurality,
cause and effect. Working with this view, some critics of the argument
from design have suggested that it fails just because, to put it as simply as
possible, order is mind-imposed rather than God-imposed.

Kant's account of categories is a long and subtle one which the reader
is urged to study for himself as a step towards assessing its relevance for
the argument from design.[7] But it is not unproblematic, and, with an eye
on the argument, there are at least two points that might be raised regarding it.

First, it is not entirely clear that Kant's account of the world and human
experience is coherent. On Kant's picture we seem to have the world as we
experience it and also something behind all this and against which the
world as we experience it is held to be some kind of construction or product
of our minds. This view involves positing a world of which we can have
no experience in order to contrast it with the world we ordinarily talk
about, and many philosophers would regard such a move as pointless. If we
can only sensibly talk about this world, then how can we believe in another
of which we cannot really talk sensibly except in the terms applicable to
this one? As one writer puts it, 'How can we talk sensibly of the existence
of a world independent of order, when to talk at all is to impose order?'[8]

It might, then, be argued that there is no clear reason for believing in
another world against which our world can be viewed as mind-imposed.
Nor do we normally believe in such a world, which brings us to a second
difficulty in regarding Kant's position as a useful weapon against the
argument from design. For if one accepts that position, one might well
wonder whether, for example, there is any particular reason to accept the
presuppositions and results of empirical inquiry. In an empirical inquiry,
such as natural science, we claim to be talking about things that are in
various ways ordered, things that would be such even if nobody could
experience them as such. We would not, for instance, normally say that
all biological analyses would cease to be true if the human race were
suddenly wiped out. But if it is rational to accept the findings and methods
of empirical inquiry, then it seems rational to accept the design argument's
premise that order is discovered, not imposed.

Hume and the design argument

To appeal to Kant's views need not, then, be taken as establishing that the
argument from design is a definite non-starter. And henceforth I shall

assume that the above replies to the view that order is mind-imposed can be used in defence of the argument from design. Many philosophers, however, would not regard Kant as a decisive critic of the design argument, for they would say that it has been successfully refuted by Hume in the *Dialogues concerning Natural Religion* and in *An Enquiry concerning Human Understanding*. Here Hume makes eight basic points against the argument from design. At this stage I shall simply introduce and briefly comment on them.

Hume's first point is one we have already come across in Chapter 5. 'When we infer any particular cause for an effect,' he says, 'we must proportion the one to the other, and can never be allowed to ascribe to any cause any qualities, but what are exactly sufficient to produce the effect.'[9] Now, Hume adds, if design needs to be explained, then explain it; but only by appealing to a design-producing being. To say that this being is God is to go beyond the evidence presented by design.

It seems to me that Hume has a strong point here. We may, of course, sometimes reasonably argue that some cause has characteristics other than those sufficient to produce some effect. If I know that X is made by a man I may reasonably say that this man has certain bodily organs and emotional capabilities, even though he would not need them to produce X. I can say this because I already know a lot about men quite apart from any inference I might make from X. But Hume is talking about a cause of order in the universe, and he is saying that if we are just confronted by order in the universe we can only ascribe to its cause whatever it needs in order to produce its effect. And, unless one already knows things about the cause of order in the universe apart from what one knows on the basis of this order, Hume's point seems correct. Coming back to God we can therefore say this. If one can reasonably say that the order in the universe needs explanation it does not follow that this explanation will be what God is said to be. Not, at any rate, unless we already know something about God and know that the explanation of order in the universe is God. God, for example, is sometimes said to be timeless; but it seems hard to see why anything capable of imposing order needs to be timeless.

Hume's second point hinges on the fact that the universe is unique. He says that 'When two *species* of objects have always been observed to be conjoined together, I can *infer*, by custom, the existence of one wherever I *see* the existence of the other; And this I call an argument from experience.'[10] According to Hume this notion of inference rules out the design argument. He writes:

But how this argument can have place, where the objects, as in the present case, are single, individual, without parallel, or specific resemblance, may be difficult to explain. And will any man tell me with a serious countenance, that an orderly universe must arise from some thought and art, like the human; because we have some experience of it? To ascertain this reasoning, it were requisite, that we had experience of the origin of worlds; and it is not sufficient surely, that we have seen ships and cities arise from human art and contrivance.[11]

At least two objections to Hume seem possible here. First, if Hume were correct then no explanation of unique things would be possible. But we normally assume otherwise. As Swinburne observes,[12] we only know of one human race, and possibly there is only one, but scientists attempt to explain its origins. As part of cosmology, they also attempt to explain the origins of the world, considered as an object of scientific inquiry, while, as far as scientific explanations of the world go, there is, presumably, only one world. Second, proponents of the design argument often deny that the universe is totally unique; they often point out that it has characteristics in common with other things. Some say, for example, that the universe as a whole resembles things like watches. If they are right here then the fact that the universe is also unique in some respect does not mean that a reasonable argument cannot be forthcoming to account for the resemblances between the universe as a whole and parts of it.

Hume's third point is that the argument from design fails to explain what it is that explains the designer for which the argument argues. 'If', says Hume, '*Reason* . . . be not alike mute with regard to all questions concerning cause and effect; this sentence at least it will venture to pronounce, That a mental world, or universe of ideas requires a cause as much as does a material world or universe of objects.'[13] Hume adds that minds depend on other things in many ways and that, 'As far as we can judge, vegetables and animal bodies are not more delicate in their motions, nor depend upon a greater variety or more curious adjustment of springs and principles.'[14] Furthermore, says Hume, positing a designer of the world leads to an infinite regression. 'If the material world rests upon a similar ideal world,' he says, 'this ideal world must rest upon some other; and so on, without end.'[15] He continues:

Naturalists indeed very justly explain particular effects by more general causes; though these general causes themselves should remain in the end totally inexplicable: But they never surely thought it satisfactory to explain a particular effect by a particular cause, which was no more to be accounted for than the effect itself. An ideal system, arranged of itself, without a precedent design, is not a whit more explicable than a material one, which attains its order in a like manner; nor is there any more difficulty in the latter supposition than in the former.[16]

What might be said in reply to Hume's third point? It seems to assume that if one explains A by B, but if one does not offer to explain B, then one has not thereby explained A. But should we accept this view? As one of the characters in Hume's *Dialogues* says, 'Even in common life, if I assign a cause for any event; is it any objection . . . that I cannot assign the cause of that cause, and answer every new question, which may incessantly be started?'[17] Even scientific explanations work within a framework where certain ultimate laws are just claimed to hold. Possibly, then, even if someone who defends the argument from design is unable to account for the existence of the designer it does not follow that he cannot argue for a designer.

But this point, even if it is correct, does not really answer Hume's objection about infinite regress. Yet this too admits of reply. For it could only be made to bite if the argument from design proposed some such premise as 'Everything exhibiting design requires a designer and every designer exhibits design.' But why should the argument propose such a premise? A defender of the argument might merely say that the universe has characteristics which make it reasonable to believe in a designer. He does not have to add that the designer has these same characteristics.

Hume's fourth point is made in the form of a question. 'And why not become a perfect anthropomorphite?' he asks. 'Why not assert the Deity or Deities to be corporeal, and to have eyes, a nose, mouth, ears, &c.?'[18] The argument here appears to be this. Some versions of the design argument argue from human artefacts to the existence of a divine intelligence supposed to account for the universe considered as one great artefact. Thus one should regard the cause of the universe's design as something in every respect like human artificers.

But this argument is not unanswerable, and there are at least two possible replies open to someone who wishes to defend some version of the design argument. First, it might be said that the designer of the universe cannot himself be corporeal without himself being part of the system of things for which the design argument proposes to account. Second, it might be pointed out that the argument from design does not have to conclude that the designer of the universe shares all the attributes of the causes whose operations provide the justification for inferring him in the first place. For some versions of the design argument are arguments from analogy, i.e. they argue from one set of known events and causes, together with another set of events, to a cause that is like, but not entirely like, the causes in question in the first case. This pattern of argument, which is very familiar in scientific theory, has been stated thus by Swinburne: 'As are caused by Bs. A*s are similar to As. Therefore – given that there is no more satisfactory explanation of the existence of A*s – they are produced by B*s similar to Bs. B*s are postulated to be similar in all respects to Bs except in so far as shown otherwise, viz., except in so far as the

dissimilarities between As and A*s force us to postulate a difference.'[19]
On the basis of this principle Swinburne proceeds to defend the argument
from design against Hume's fourth point. He writes:

For the activity of a god to account for the regularities, he must be free, rational,
and very powerful. But it is not necessary that he, like men, should only be able to
act on a limited part of the universe, a body, and by acting on that control the rest
of the universe. And there is good reason to suppose that the god does not operate
in this way. For, if his direct control was confined to a part of the universe, scientific
laws outside his control must operate to ensure that his actions have effects in the
rest of the universe. Hence the postulation of the existence of the god would not
explain the operations of those laws: yet to explain the operation of all scientific laws
was the point of postulating the existence of the god. The hypothesis that the god
is not embodied thus explains more and explains more coherently than the
hypothesis that he is embodied.[20]

In his next point Hume suggests that the defender of the argument from
design has no reason for denying that there may not be a whole gang of
gods working together to produce design in the universe. 'A great number
of men', he says, 'join together in building a house or ship, in rearing a city,
in framing a commonwealth: Why may not several Deities combine in
contriving and framing a world?'[21]

This point has a certain strength, for design is often the work of many
individuals. But there is still the famous philosophical principle commonly called 'Ockham's razor', according to which 'Entities are not to be
multiplied beyond necessity.' It is often said that this principle should
govern all serious speculation about the existence of things. A defender of
the argument from design might therefore argue that, though there is
reason to believe in one designer god, there is no reason to believe in more
than one, though there might possibly be more than one. In this connection it is, perhaps, worth noting that Hume himself seems to accept a
version of Ockham's razor. 'To multiply causes, without necessity,' he
says, 'is indeed contrary to true philosophy.'[22]

Let us now pass quickly on to Hume's last three points. The first is that
the universe might easily be regarded as a living organism such as a plant,
in which case the argument from design fails since it depends on compar-
ing the universe to a machine or artefact of some kind. The next point is
that the order in the universe might easily be the result of chance. The final
point is that the argument from design fails because the universe shows
plenty of signs of disorder.

Are Hume's arguments here decisive? It seems to me that it is certainly
possible to doubt that they are.

Even if we press the analogy between the universe and a living organism,
we still seem confronted by regularity in the universe. I have said little

about this so far but now it can be argued that the universe seems to behave in regular and predictable ways. As Swinburne observes, 'the universe is characterized by vast, all-pervasive temporal order, the conformity of nature to formula, recorded in the scientific laws formulated by men. . . . The orderliness of the universe to which I draw attention here is its conformity to formula, to simple, formulable, scientific laws. The order-liness of the universe in this respect is a very striking fact about it. The universe might so naturally have been chaotic, but it is not – it is very orderly.'[23] Now it seems open to the defender of the design argument to draw attention to what Swinburne is talking about and to point out the similarity between machines and the universe. For it is characteristic of a machine that it behaves in regular and predictable ways and obeys scienti-fic laws. He might even add that his appeal to a designer helps to explain more than an appeal to the generative power of living organisms in ac-counting for the order in the universe, an appeal which Hume seems to be making in suggesting that the analogy between the universe and an organ-ism is a problem for the argument from design. For living organisms reproduce regularity because they are already things that display it. Thus it might be said that living organisms cannot explain all the regularity in the universe since they depend on some form of regularity themselves.

Hume's point about chance is that over the course of eternity there will be times of order and times of chaos, so that the universe may once have been in chaos and the present ordered universe may derive from this state. In reply to this point, however, it might be said that Hume is only noting a logical possibility which need not affect the fact that the universe is not now in chaos, which calls for explanation. It might also be said that an explanation of the universe which excludes the role of chance grows more credible as time goes by. Thus Swinburne suggests that 'If we say that it is chance that in 1960 matter is behaving in a regular way, our claim becomes less and less plausible as we find that in 1961 and 1962 and so on it continues to behave in a regular way.'[24]

But what of Hume's final point? Certainly it might be said that in one sense it is clearly right: the universe contains disorder since there are, for example, pain-producing events of a natural kind. But this fact need not deter the defender of the argument from design unless he wishes to hold that every particular thing works to the advantage of other particular things, which he may well not wish to do. He may only want to say that there is order in need of explanation; and disorder *qua* pain-producing natural events can plausibly be taken as just an illustration of order. One might, for instance, argue that pain-producing natural events exhibit order in that their origins can often be traced and their future occurrence predicted with a fair degree of success.

Is the argument from design reasonable?

It seems, then, that, if they are taken individually, most of Hume's arguments against the design argument admit of reply. But a defender of Hume might accept this conclusion and still urge that Hume has knocked a massive hole in the argument. Consider the following imaginary dialogue:

A. Brown has stabbed Jones to death.
B. Prove that.
A. Brown had a motive.
B. That does not prove that Brown stabbed Jones. Many people had a motive for killing Jones.
A. Brown was found at the scene of the crime.
B. That fact is compatible with his innocence.
A. Brown was found standing over Jones holding a blood-stained knife.
B. He may have picked it up after the murder was committed.
A. Brown says he stabbed Jones.
B. He may be trying to cover up for somebody.

Now B's points here, taken individually, are all quite correct. But when A's points are taken together, and though it may still be that A is wrong about Brown, a reasonable person would surely conclude that they put a pretty hefty question mark over Brown's innocence. Might it not similarly be said that Hume's arguments, if not all decisive individually, make it unreasonable to accept the argument from design?

Evidently, a great deal turns here on the initial strength of the design argument. In reading the above dialogue one would tend to disregard B's points because of the way in which A's points seem to point one way when taken together. In the same way, if the argument from design could be stated in such a way as to point towards an external (or, as some would put it, 'extra-mundane') cause of order in the universe, then that would make it reasonable to accept the argument and continue to insist that Hume's case against it is not compelling. Is it, then, possible to regard the argument from design as an independently strong argument?

Common to all versions of the argument are two suggestions:

(1) The universe contains a high degree of order.
(2) It is reasonable to account for this order with reference to an external and intelligent cause, i.e. a cause that is intelligent but not part of the ordered universe.

Are these suggestions reasonable?

(1) has already concerned us in discussion of Hume. And in the light of that discussion I would suggest that (1) is true. The universe does contain

a high degree of order in that scientific laws can be framed and expectations reasonably made about the behaviour of things over a very wide area. Even when we cannot formulate a law for accounting for some phenomenon we tend to assume that there is one.

(2) is certainly open to the reply that while we may think that order requires explanation of a certain kind there is no guarantee that there is any such explanation. Our expectations regarding what must account for what may prove unfulfilled in perhaps all cases. But it is not always reasonable to speculate on the basis of this possibility. And when we are confronted with orderly arrangements of things where there might have been chaos, and unless we have positive evidence that no intelligence has brought them about, we simply do seek to account for them with reference to intelligence. Numbers on a set of fifty pages could be set down in a totally random way; but once we discover that they can be regularly translated into something strongly resembling a language, we presume that we are dealing with a code. Bits of machinery could be piled up in a formless and inert heap; but when we come across bits that operate together with each other so as to do something repeatedly and predictably, we presume that they form some kind of artefact. Musical notes could be written down in a totally random way; but if they can be read so as to produce a symphony when played, we call the notes a score.

In other words, unless we have a definite reason for ruling out explanation with reference to intelligent agency it is reasonable to postulate such agency when confronted by order when there could have been chaos, i.e. when it is consistent to suppose that the existence of the order is not logically necessary. But if this is so, and unless we have a definite reason for ruling out explanation with reference to intelligent agency, then it seems reasonable to postulate intelligent agency when confronted by the order in the universe. For that might never have been there at all and yet is there to a high degree. It may, of course, be said that the order in the universe is just there and is not the product of intelligence. But granted that we normally attempt to account for order in terms of intelligence when we lack a definite reason for doing otherwise, such a reply seems arbitrary. A supporter of Hume might say that when we postulate intelligence in accounting for order we only do so when we are confronted by examples of what we know to be normally produced by intelligence. But that is just what the argument from design can be said to do. As we saw earlier, it can be seen as appealing to the fact that the ordered universe taken as a whole is not unique in that it shares characteristics with its parts of such a kind as to make it reasonable to say that if intelligence can be invoked to account for what is true of these parts then intelligence can be invoked to account for what is similarly true of the whole. And the intelligence in question will clearly have to be extra-mundane. For it is the whole mundane order that would have to be accounted for by it. As Swinburne puts it, the pervasive temporal order in the universe

is clearly something 'too big' to be explained by science. If there is an explanation of the world's order it cannot be a scientific one, and this follows from the nature of scientific explanation. . . . In scientific explanation we explain particular phenomena as brought about by prior phenomena in accord with scientific laws; or we explain the operation of scientific laws in terms of more general scientific laws (and perhaps also particular phenomena). . . . Science thus explains particular phenomena and low-level laws in terms partly of high-level laws. But from the very nature of science it cannot explain the very highest-level laws of all; for they are that by which it explains all other phenomena.[25]

But might it not be said that there is definite reason for ruling out explanation of the universe's order with reference to intelligence? The trouble is that it seems hard to know what kind of reason this could be. When we allow that a certain kind of order is definitely not to be explained with reference to intelligence we already know that some natural laws and not intelligence have brought it about. Thus we can deny intelligent causation of the ridges in the sand which remain when the tide has gone out because we can definitely account for them with reference to physical laws such as those which govern the movement of wind and waves. But in the case of the order in the universe it is precisely in physical laws that the order to be accounted for resides. This means that any proffered reason for ruling out intelligent causation of the order in the universe would have to take the form of a proof to the effect that the notion of extra-mundane intelligent agency is logically impossible. But two points need to be made in this connection.

The first is that if there is such a proof, it is by no means universally acknowledged. As we shall see in Chapter 12, some philosophers have views about mind and body that would lead them to reject as unintelligible the notion that there could be mind without body. It would be in reliance on such a view that one would have to try to show that extra-mundane intelligent agency is logically impossible. But the mind–body debate is not a topic on which there is universal agreement among philosophers. For this reason it may fairly be said that, at present at least, it is rash to assume that there is proof of the impossibility of extra-mundane intelligence.

The second point concerns grounds for concluding that something is logically impossible. Sometimes it is self-evident that a statement is logically impossible. This is the case with 'There is a figure which is simultaneously perfectly round and perfectly square.' But some statements are not so easy to decide upon. Examples include 'A cause can follow its effect', 'Time travel is possible', and 'Only something with a body can be intelligent.' Now one way of trying to settle the issue of these statements is to indicate some possible good reason for thinking that what they claim to be possible is somehow exemplified. Thus, for instance, Michael Dummett tries to spell out conditions which would, if they held, give good reason to believe that an event at time 3 was the cause of an event at time 2.[26] So sometimes the possibility of giving a good reason for holding that-P can be taken as evidence that P is logically possible. But, returning to the design argument, it does seem that there is reason for holding that there is an extra-mundane intelligent cause of the order in the universe. There is therefore reason for holding that such a cause is logically possible. Notice that if one accepted this conclusion one would be working with the view of analogical use of language presented in Chapter 2. For the argument from design is saying that 'intelligent' can be applied both to things in the world and to what brings it about that there is the order which we find in the world without it meaning the same on both occasions, yet without it meaning something entirely different. And it is saying this because it holds that there are reasons for applying the word in this way.

The argument from design and God

At the end of Chapter 5 we saw that there was no reason to believe that the cosmological argument provides grounds for believing that the cause of the existence of things can be identified with God, at least in so far as 'God' bears the meaning it does for people like classical theists. I have now suggested that the argument from design is a reasonable argument for the view that the order in the universe is caused by intelligence. But does this mean that the argument is enough to justify belief in something like the God of classical theism?

Clearly if the argument from design shows that one can reasonably hold that the order in the universe is brought about by intelligence then it shows that one can reasonably regard the cause of the universe's order as conscious and knowledgeable in some sense. For if X is unconscious all the time then X cannot do anything that would allow one to call it intelligent. And if X's action allows one to call X intelligent then X must have knowledge since the notion of something intelligent but lacking in any knowledge seems contradictory. Furthermore, if X is the intelligent cause of a vast degree of order it seems reasonable to suppose that X is very knowledgeable and also very powerful. It can therefore be said that what the argument from design leads to has something in common with the theistic God.

But the theistic God is said to be the cause of the existence of things and to be unique, and the question arises as to whether by itself the argument from design gives any reason to believe that the theistic God exists in this sense. I think the answer has to be that by itself it does not. For it is not necessary that X should be the cause of the existence of Y even though it is the cause of order that Y exhibits. But if we adopt the principle of Ockham's razor it may, as I said above, be argued that one can reasonably hold that the cause of the order in the universe is single rather than plural. Certainly this argument would leave one with a more economical hypothesis than Hume's suggestion that the order in the world is the result of many gods collaborating together. As Swinburne fairly observes: 'Hume's hypothesis is very complicated – we want to ask about it such questions as why are there just 333 deities (or whatever the number is), why do they have powers of just the strength which they do have, and what moves them to co-operate as closely as obviously they do.'[27]

We have, then, some reason for refusing to postulate a number of causes for the order in the universe. But any attempt to identify the cause of the order in the universe with the theistic God would still have to cope with the possibility that what causes the universe's order does not bring things into existence.

At this point, however, a further move is open to someone who thinks that the argument from design can be invoked in the context of a discussion about the existence of God. For if one already has reason to believe that the existence of things is caused in the way that the cosmological argument suggests, there is very good reason indeed for identifying the first cause spoken of in the cosmological argument with the cause of the universe's order spoken of in the argument from design. For if one accepts both arguments as far as they take one, one has an alternative. Drawing on what was said in Chapter 5, it seems fair to say that someone who accepts the cosmological argument reasonably believes that there is a cause of all existing things, a cause which cannot be said to be duplicated, a cause which is very powerful and possibly timeless. Drawing on what has been said in this chapter, it seems fair to say that someone who accepts the argument from design reasonably believes that there is an intelligent cause of the order in the universe, a cause which can be called conscious and knowledgeable and very powerful, a cause which one has reason to say is unique. If one accepts both the cosmological and design arguments one will therefore have to say either (A) that there are two distinguishable causes, one as concluded to by the cosmological argument and one as concluded to in the argument from design, or (B) that the cause of all existing things is also the cause of the order in the universe.

Now which of these alternatives is the more reasonable? One might say (A) on the ground that (B) is unprovable. But if the cosmological argument is correct, and if (A) is accepted, then that to which the cosmological argument concludes must be the cause of that to which the argument from design concludes. For if the cause of order in the universe is not itself the cause of existing things then it might never have existed at all, and if it does exist then, in terms of the cosmological argument, its existence is caused.

If, then, one accepts (A) one will have to draw together the cause of the universe's order and the cause of existing things. And the implications of doing so are interesting. For the very being of the cause of the universe's order will be due to the cause of existing things, which means that, given the cosmological and design arguments, the reality of the order in the universe is attributable to the first cause of existence, in which case it is true to say of the cause of existing things that it is the cause of the order in the universe. And that surely makes it more reasonable to prefer (B) to (A). In other words, there is reason for saying that the cause of existing things is the cause of the order in the universe, while apart from the fact that a cause of order need not be a cause of existence, there seems no reason for saying that the cause of the order in the universe is not the cause of the existence of things. In preferring (B) to (A) one is therefore preferring the presence of a reason to the absence of one. And in doing so one would be saying that it is reasonable to hold that there is a cause of the existence of things which (a) cannot be said to be duplicated, (b) brings about the order in the universe, (c) is very powerful, knowledgeable, intelligent, and possibly timeless.

How far does such a suggestion take one in the context of the question of God's existence? If we work with the notion of God present in classical theism, it must surely be allowed that even if it is not identical with the assertion that there is a God it is yet remarkably close to what seems to be meant by that assertion. In other words, in preferring (B) one would be saying something which seems to go a very long way towards agreeing with the theistic assertion that there is a God. If, then the cosmological and design arguments are reasonable, and if they are brought together, it seems reasonable to say that reasonable argument for God's existence is, after all, possible. I have been arguing that the cosmological and design arguments are reasonable, so I suggest now that reasonable argument for God's existence is possible. The reader, of course, may disagree. But at least he now has something with which to disagree.

7 Experience and God

It should be clear enough by now how various people have held that argument can be offered to show that it is reasonable to say that there is a God. But it has also been held that the reasonableness of belief in God can be defended not with reference to argument but with reference to experience, and it is to this view that I now wish to turn. The question currently at issue is therefore this: does experience tell a reasonable man that God exists?

God and experience

To begin with we had better ask what is meant by saying that it is reasonable to believe in God on the basis of experience. Perhaps the answer can be given by means of a contrast.

The arguments for God which I have discussed so far evidently suppose that a reasonable belief in God can be arrived at through some kind of medium. The ontological argument finds this in the definition of the word 'God'. According to the cosmological and design arguments the medium is the universe and the way it operates. For all these arguments it seems to be a question of getting to God through something else, of finding out that there is a God because something other than God's existence happens to be the case.

But we do not always justify our beliefs about the way things are in such an indirect way. When Mabel stares lovingly into Fred's eyes she does not talk of her indirect way of knowing that Fred is there. She would probably say that she was just aware of Fred. And something similar might be said by someone listening to a piece of music. Albert listens to the Eroica Symphony and regards it as a fine piece of music. But Albert might hold that he does not conclude that the Eroica is fine because he has followed any kind of argument. He may simply say that its value is directly present to him, that it is something discovered without argument, something seen, not inferred.

Now it is this kind of example that helps one to see what appeal to experience of God is getting at. The idea is that just as Mabel can be directly aware of Fred, and just as Albert can be directly aware of the valuable nature of the Eroica, so it is possible to be directly aware of God. On this account it is not necessary to think of there having to be anything between a person and God; someone can just know, just see, that God is there. Mabel knows that Fred is there because she experiences his presence; Albert may say that he knows that the Eroica is valuable just in listening to the music. In the same way it has been said that one can experience or be directly aware of God. In other words, the claim is that without appealing to anything other than a direct contact with God one can have reasonable grounds for asserting that there is a God. Just as I can reasonably say that there is a bed in my room because I have encountered it, so I can reasonably say that there is a God because I have directly encountered him.

Objections to the above view

A number of reasons have been given for rejecting the view that God can be reasonably said to exist since there is direct awareness or experience of him. To begin with I shall simply reproduce without comment those most often advanced.

1. Experience cannot be taken as giving reasonable grounds for belief in God since the notion of God is an impossible one. There could not be a God and therefore there could not be an experience of God.

2. Experience is frequently deceptive. We often say that we are aware of X or that we experience the presence of X when argument or further experience forces us to conclude that we are mistaken. Thus we note the whole area of mistaken identification (taking Jones for Smith), misinterpretation of evidence (regarding converging railway lines as really meeting), and hallucination (seeing objects which are not there to be seen). Any claim based on experience is therefore suspect.

3. There are too many reasons for doubting that when a person says he experiences God he actually does so. Someone who claims an experience of God may be mistakenly identifying the object of his experience, or he may be hallucinating or insane. Furthermore, anyone claiming an experience of God is probably only influenced by some psychological or social pressure leading him to believe that there is a God. In any case, any proclaimed experience of God must be rejected *ab initio* (*a*) because there are no agreed tests for verifying that there has in fact been an experience of God, and (*b*) because some people report an experience of the absence of God or because there is no uniformity of testimony on the part of those who claim to experience God.

Are the objections decisive?

Let us for the moment consider the merits of the above objections individually. Does any of them show that it cannot be reasonable to believe in God on the basis of experience?

The first objection can, perhaps, be fairly quickly dealt with at this stage. More often than not it reflects the views of people who think that God's existence is intrinsically impossible. I considered some questions relevant to this view in Chapters 1–3 and I argued that they do not show that there could not be a God. Furthermore, it is possible, as I argued in Chapters 5 and 6, to offer a reasonable case that takes one a long way towards theism. So it is at least not evident that there could not be a God and therefore not evident that there could not be a reasonable belief in God based on experience just because there could not be a God.

Nor is it evident that any claim that something is so is suspect if it is based on experience. Claims based on experience may be withdrawn by the people who make them, but this fact does not show that they can never be correct. The argument from the fact of revision cannot be used to deny in some absolute sense the possibility of knowing by experience. Fred may hallucinate when under the influence of drink, and he may emphatically state that there is a goblin in the room. Subsequently he may withdraw his statement. When under the influence again, however, he may withdraw his retraction. The fact that we would normally ignore his second retraction is evidence for our conviction that retraction by itself settles nothing about the truth of what is retracted.

Furthermore, even if it is possible to be mistaken with a claim based on experience, not all such claims need be mistaken. A general argument from illusion, from the possibility of mistaken identification or misinterpretation of evidence, cannot always be rationally used in assessing the correctness of all assertions based on experience that something is the case. Context is very important here. It might be reasonable to challenge Fred's assertion about the goblin, but if I am assured by my doctors to be in good health, with normal eyesight, of average sanity and intelligence, it might well be unreasonable for me to doubt that when I seem to see a train bearing down upon me at the crossing there really is such a thing. We need to remember the implications involved in our notions of mistaken identity, misinterpretation of evidence, and hallucination. Mistakenly to identify X is to have an experience of X and erroneously to believe that X is something other than X. It must therefore be possible to have an experience of X and correctly to believe that it is X. To misinterpret evidence is to be aware of something and to draw mistaken conclusions about it. It must therefore be possible to be aware of something and to draw correct conclusions about it. To have an hallucination is mistakenly to believe that something is present to one. It must therefore be possible to believe correctly that something is present to one.

In short, there seems good reason to say that some claims can be reasonably upheld on the basis of experience. Sometimes one may just have to say that one sees that something is the case. And, of course, if one could not reasonably do this then one could not even reasonably say that the objections made against claims based on experience are worth taking seriously. For how does one know that there are any such objections? Only by listening to people make them or by reading about them in books, i.e. by supposing that at least some things that seem directly given to one in one's experience are there in reality. We certainly do make mistakes about reality because we fail to interpret our experience correctly; but if we do not work on the assumption that what seems to be so is sometimes so, then it is hard to see how we can establish anything at all and how we can correct beliefs that are in some way mistaken. Rational inquiry seems to presuppose that it is reasonable to say that what directly seems to be so is so. One might argue that this cannot be so since in a truly rational inquiry one can accept nothing unless it is justified on independent grounds. Yet justification for propositions cannot always be provided. In *On Certainty* Wittgenstein brings this fact out very well. 'Doesn't testing come to an end?' he asks rhetorically.[1] 'The difficulty', he continues, 'is to realize the groundlessness of our believing.'[2] By way of example he cites the case of the chemist:

Think of chemical investigations. Lavoisier makes experiments with substances in his laboratory and now he concludes that this and that takes place when there is burning. He does not say that it might happen otherwise another time. He has got hold of a definite world picture — not of course one that he invented: he learned it as a child. I say world-picture and not hypothesis, because it is the matter-of-course foundation for his research and as such also goes unmentioned.[3]

Wittgenstein's point is not that we are sometimes not clever enough to justify our beliefs; he is saying that before you raise questions of justification you have to accept some things without question. As he puts it himself: 'At the foundation of well-founded belief lies belief that is not founded. . . . Justification by experience comes to an end. If it did not it would not be justification. . . . If I have exhausted the justifications I have reached bedrock, and my spade is turned. Then I am inclined to say: "This is simply what I do." '[4]

A similar kind of argument to that of the last few paragraphs can be used in reply to the third objection to the view that belief in God can be reasonably based on experience. We must surely admit in general terms that if a person claims an experience of God he may be mistakenly identifying the object of his experience. Since it seems reasonable to believe that people sometimes hallucinate and are sometimes insane, and since it seems reasonable to believe that it is possible to believe things because of psychological or social pressures, one must, presumably, also allow that it is possible that a particular claim to experience of God may spring only from hallucination, insanity, or the effects of psychological or social pressures. But several points need to be added.

From 'It is usually or often or sometimes the case that-P' we cannot deduce that it is always the case that-P. So Fred may be as mad as a hatter and as drunk as a lord, and it may still be true that on some particular occasion Fred got it right and was reasonable in believing something on the basis of experience. Furthermore, the truth of a belief is not affected by the factors that bring the belief about. Suppose that Fred says he believes in God on the basis of experience, and suppose that some psychologist or sociologist can produce a plausible account of how Fred got into the state of believing in God. It still does not follow that Fred is wrong or that his experience can never give him grounds for asserting that something is the case.

If, then, we point to possibilities of hallucination and so forth, perhaps the most we can demand is a bias in favour of disregarding particular claims to experience God. Given clear evidence that Fred normally misinterprets the objects of his experience, that he regularly hallucinates, that he is insane or largely influenced by psychological or social pressures, it might be reasonable to conclude that he is probably mistaken on any given occasion. If a man regularly hallucinates he regularly believes that things exist when they do not. One might therefore argue that it is possible that for any further claim of his that something is the case he is mistaken.

But can this point show that no person can reasonably believe in God on the basis of his experience? Since it appeals to special cases the answer must be No. But someone may say that we have good reason to believe that all people who claim to have experienced God are unreliable because they regularly hallucinate, are insane, and so on. But is this suggestion plausible? It seems difficult to see that it is, since many people who have seemed to claim some kind of experience of God are people whom one would normally regard as sane and reliable. One thinks here of famous mystical authors like Teresa of Avila (1515–82), John of the Cross (1542–91) and Walter Hilton (d. *c*.1395).[5] It would be widely accepted, even by those with no belief in God, that in the writings of these people we find strong evidence of accurate perception and depth of insight.

It may be said, however, that there are no agreed tests for distinguishing experience of God from illusion or mistaken identification. And it would often be urged that if something is said to be the case it must be possible to state tests which can be conducted by several people as a means of confirmation. Some philosophers would add that these tests must be empirical, and they would argue that since God is not an empirical entity it follows that experience of God can never be claimed to have occurred.

But these points are not enough to discredit the view that one can reasonably believe in God on the basis of experience. First the truth of a claim that something is the case is independent of any agreed tests used to corroborate it. Second, there are grounds for denying that any possibly true claim that something is so must be a statement of empirical fact confirmable in principle empirically. Here I would refer the reader back to the discussion of Chapter 1.

In addition to these points there is something further that needs to be said about the question of agreed tests and experience of God. For are there really no agreed tests for picking out a genuine experience of God? Not everyone agrees about what would count in favour of a claim to have experienced God, but it is hard to know what claims are such that everybody agrees about what counts in their favour. If, then, we are to speak about agreed tests being required in order for one to be reasonable in making a certain claim, we cannot demand that the agreement involved be universal; not, at least, without putting a question mark over many assertions that may well be rationally believed. And once this point is allowed it seems far from clear that there are no agreed tests for distinguishing a genuine experience of God from something else. Those who believe that there actually is experience of God frequently say something about its effects on the experient, the content of the experience, and the results to be expected in the behaviour of the experient. It is said, for example, that an experience of God is accompanied by a unique sense of humility, of creatureliness, of fear and awe mingled with a strong sense of passivity and dependence. The object of the experience is usually said to be holy, awful, loving and so on. It is commonly accepted that an experience of God will lead people to some kind of conversion of manners or to some kind of change of attitude or increased perspicacity. One may not think that any of these points shows that experience of God is a fact; but at present we are asking whether there are any agreed tests regarding experience of God. And it seems that there are.

We come, then, to the observation that people sometimes report an experience of the absence of God and that those who claim an experience of God give no uniform testimony concerning the nature and object of their experience. But these observations do not get us very far either. Indeed there are people who say that they are struck by the absence of God in their experience. And there are people who never give the notion of God a second thought. But the fact that some people's account of their experience does not square with other people's account of theirs does not, by itself, establish that one of the accounts is wrong. A number of people may have good evidence that a certain animal is to be found in the jungle because they have seen it. Let us suppose that a second group of people go into the jungle to look for the animal in question. They search for a very long time but they do not find it. Can we conclude from this that the first group of people did not have reasonable grounds for affirming that the animal was actually there? Obviously not. And, if 'uniformity of testimony' means 'absolute agreement', then there is no reason to believe that no claim to have experienced God can be a rational one because those who claim experience of God do not provide uniformity of testimony concerning the nature and object of their experience. Three points might be noted here.

First, it makes sense to say that some claims based on experience can be reasonably made while there is no absolute agreement concerning the nature and object of their experience on the part of those who defend the claim. Two astronomers can agree about the existence of a star and they can be reasonable in holding that it exists though they see it from different locations and with different instruments. And two doctors can be presented with a virus and be reasonable in believing in its existence without agreeing about its nature.

Second, if A and B claim on the basis of experience that something is the case, but if they also disagree about the nature of the experience and the nature of what is experienced, it does not follow that one of them cannot be right and the other wrong and that one of them cannot be reasonable in making his claim and the other unreasonable.

Third, the fact that A and B disagree about the nature of X which, so they say, they have experienced, need not show that both of them cannot be right in claiming that X is there and that it is reasonable to believe so. To show this it would have to be established that A and B ascribed properties to X that are logically incompatible if predicated of one thing.

Experience as a reason for belief in God

The conclusion to be drawn from the above reflections would seem to be that the objections which we have noted to the view that one can reasonably believe in God on the basis of experience are not decisive when taken individually. There might be a God; even though appeal to experience is not always a guarantee of infallibility it is sometimes reasonable to defend claims with reference to experience; people who claim experience of God seem reasonable in other respects; and it is possible to speak of agreed tests for identifying experience of God.

But this is not to say that it is ever reasonable to believe in God on the basis of experience of God. And at this stage I should wish to argue that there are considerations that ought at least to make us suspicious of the view that it is.

The major problem concerns the supposed object of an experience of God. If one is disposed to say that a seeming experience of X can be a reason for believing in X one might say that a seeming experience of God is a reason for believing in God. And if one already has reason for thinking that there is a God one might argue that someone's claim to have experienced God is all the more credible. If there is a God, one might say, it is likely that he would communicate himself to people directly. But the claim that it is reasonable to believe in God on the basis of experience is heavily dependent on the notion of coming across something in the world. This is thought to be similar to experience of God in that it involves a direct contact between the experient and something outside himself. Just as Mabel can be directly aware of Fred so, it is said, people can be directly aware of God.

But the trouble with this suggestion is that God is usually said to be very different from any particular thing which we might come across in our day-to-day lives. As I argued earlier, it can even be said that God is not any particular thing at all. If he were then he would not be the cause of the existence of all things. In other words it seems reasonable to say that if any experience of God occurred at all it could not be the experience of any particular thing. But the claim that it is reasonable to believe in God on the basis of experience seems to be arguing differently. For it compares the experience of God to the experience (the coming across or into contact with) of particular things.

Now it might be objected that there is nothing in the notion of an experience of X that shows that it must be the notion of an experience of something particular. And up to a point this is a plausible objection. It seems possible to substitute for 'experience' words like 'see' or 'perceive'. Thus to say that I know Fred by experience is to say that I have seen Fred or that I have perceived him. Yet not all seeing or perceiving is seeing or perceiving something particular. We talk of seeing the point of an argument, of seeing what someone means, of seeing that something is going to happen. But we surely cannot maintain that the point of an argument is a particular thing. And the same goes for what someone means and what is going to happen. Take also the case of seeing that there is blindness. It seems plausible to suggest that we can see that there is blindness; one might even talk about one's experience of blindness or one's contact with it. But blindness is not a thing, a kind of appendage that blind people have in the same way that they might have a cancerous growth or a forty-inch waist. When we say that blindness is, what we really mean is that something is not, i.e. the power of sight. It seems, then, that we can talk of seeing without referring to the picking out of a particular thing, which suggests that there is quite a complexity in the use of terms like 'see' and 'experience'. Someone might therefore say that there need be nothing wrong in principle with the suggestion that one can see or experience God but that God is not a particular thing. If I can see the point of an argument without its being true that I am seeing a particular thing, why may it not be possible to see God? Why can I not experience the presence of God just as I experience the presence of blindness?

But this line of argument is a very poor defence of the view that it can be reasonable to believe in God on the basis of experience. For surely belief in God is something very different from belief in the point of an argument, belief in what someone means, belief in what is going to happen, and belief that there is blindness. And those who defend the rationality of belief in God with reference to experience seem to recognize this. Presumably that is why they often draw a comparison between experience of God and experience of the presence of a person. But if we now concentrate on this comparison we can see that it does little to justify the idea that it is called in to illustrate. For people are particular things which can be picked out and distinguished from other kinds of things.

According to some of those who appeal to it, our experience of other people can be compared to experience of God because it involves an awareness of what is non-empirical. People, it is said, are more than their bodies; they have a non-empirical or non-material side to them. How do we know them then? Not, so it is argued, by inference; rather by a direct awareness of the non-empirical side of people which is mediated by their bodies. Thus it is said that there is a good analogy for experience of God, viz. our experience of the non-empirical side of people.

In fact, however, the analogy is very weak indeed. One reason is that any human being is a particular thing and God, so it can be said, is not such. Secondly, what we know of people's presence is not something gained independently of their physical presence and behaviour. Even if thinking, for example, is not just a material process, it is still true that I can only know that you are thinking if you give some overt indication of doing so, e.g. by looking pensive, by muttering arguments, and so on. If you stand like a statue all through your life I will have no more reason to ascribe thoughts to you than I do to the Venus de Milo. We do not just learn of a person's mental life or non-empirical nature independently of their bodily presence and behaviour. In the same way, if the comparison between God and a person is pressed, we cannot just learn of God's existence independently of his bodily behaviour. The trouble is, though, God is not supposed to have a body. So how can we come across him in a way analogous to that by which we come across persons?

It might be said that in the case of God one comes across him in and through his effects, i.e. in and through the universe. But if one does say this how would one's position differ from that of someone who argues that it is reasonable to believe in God because there are arguments such as the cosmological and design ones? As far as I can see, if one insisted that there was a difference one would have to say that in the case of an experience of God there is no inference or argument involved. One just directly knows, sees, or apprehends God through the universe, as if the universe was like a window through which one could gaze into God.

A number of writers have spoken in this way. A good example is H. D. Lewis: 'We seem to see that in the last resort the world just could not exist by some extraordinary chance or just happen . . . all that we encounter points to a Reality which is complete and self-contained and which is the ultimate ground or condition of all the conditioned limited reality we find ourselves and the world around us to be.'[6] In this connection Lewis refers to 'one leap of thought in which finite and infinite are equally present and which cannot be broken up into steps which we may negotiate one by one'.[7] We have here a sense of contingency, 'not just a feeling . . . but a conviction or insight, a sense that something must be, a cognition in more technical terms'.[8]

Perhaps there is a place in rational argument for a simple, unargued-for assertion that something is so. If one wishes to give a great deal of weight to this conclusion one may say that Lewis's position is intelligible and indicates that one may reasonably believe in God on the basis of experience. But it is still a very obscure position. For one thing it is hard to know what the object of Lewis's supposed cognition can be. How would one recognize the infinite if one came across it? But just as baffling is Lewis's way of expressing his position. He evidently regards it as registering the reality of a direct experience of God, but the language he uses in presenting it is not that which we associate with talk about direct experience of something real (on the analogy of A being directly aware of B and so on). That employs expressions like 'I came across' or 'I encountered'. Lewis, on the other hand, talks about what we see must be so 'in the last resort', something that connects up with our views about what can and cannot happen by chance. He also talks about everything 'pointing' to something and of sensing 'that something must be'. Surely, however, if one sees 'in the last resort' that something can or cannot happen by chance one is drawing on a whole deposit of ideas, possibilities, reasons, and so forth. And if A points to B then surely A is distinct from B and B is inferred on the basis of A. Finally, if we see that something *must* be we surely have a complex thought and not just an encounter or coming across. To say that something must be is to say that the contrary assertion is absurd or is some kind of affront to reason. And this is not at all the same as saying that one has just come across something. When a man is hit by a car he does not talk of seeing that something must be. His talk about what must be comes at a later stage and is based on a complex pattern of inference which itself depends on a background knowledge of various things that is not simply derived from his encounter with the car. What Lewis refers to as an experience of God is much more like being convinced that something is the case than just coming across something, and it is not at all clear that this is different from seeing that arguments like the cosmological and design arguments are compelling.

A position related to that of Lewis is offered by John Hick who takes as his starting-point some passages in Wittgenstein's *Philosophical Investigations*.[9] Here Wittgenstein discusses the notion of seeing, and he observes that there are different senses of the word 'see'. One kind of seeing that interests him is that kind where, having looked at something for a while, a new aspect of it dawns on us, even though what we have been looking at has not itself changed. The example he cites is the psychologists' picture (Jastrow's 'duck-rabbit') which, when looked at, sometimes appears to people to be a picture of a duck and sometimes a picture of a rabbit.

It is from this picture, and others like it, that Hick takes his cue. We can, he says, often see things now in one way, now in another, even though what we have been looking at does not really change. What changes is the way we see things. But, Hick adds, *all* perception or seeing or experience of things is really like this. In other words, all experience is a matter of 'seeing-as'. He writes:

It is today hardly a contentious doctrine requiring elaborate argumentation that seeing . . . is not a simple matter of physical objects registering themselves on our retinas and thence in our conscious visual fields. . . . We speak of seeing-as when that which is objectively there, in the sense of that which affects the retina, can be consciously perceived in two different ways as having two different characters or natures or meanings or significances. . . . We perceive and recognize by means of all the relevant senses co-operating as a single complex means of perception; and I suggest that we use the term 'experiencing-as' to refer to the end product of this in consciousness . . . *all* experiencing is experiencing-as. . . . To recognize or identify is to experience-as in terms of a concept; and our concepts are social products having their life within a particular linguistic environment . . . all conscious experiencing involves recognitions which go beyond what is given to the senses and is thus a matter of experiencing-as.[10]

From this conclusion Hick moves to the suggestion that someone who believes in God can be regarded as experiencing everything as something behind which God lies. Believers see the world as a world where God is present. And, since all experience is experience-as, their position is no worse than anyone else's. 'The analogy to be explored', says Hick,

is with two contrasting ways of experiencing the events of our lives and of human history, on the one hand as purely natural events and on the other as mediating the presence and activity of God. For there is a sense in which the religious man and the atheist both live in the same world and another sense in which they live consciously in different worlds. They inhabit the same physical environment and are confronted by the same changes occurring within it. But in its actual concrete character in their respective 'streams of consciousness' it has for each a different nature and quality, a different meaning and significance; for one does and the other does not experience life as a continual interaction with the transcendent God . . . ordinary secular perceiving shares a common epistemological character with religious experiencing . . . all conscious perceiving goes beyond what the senses report to a significance which has not as such been given to the senses. And the religious experience of life as a sphere in which we have continually to do with God and he with us is likewise an awareness in our experience as a whole of a significance which transcends the scope of the senses. . . . We have learned, starting from scratch, to identify rabbits and forks and innumerable other kinds of thing. And so there is thus far in principle no difficulty about the claim that we may learn to use the concept 'act of God', as we have learned to use other concepts, and acquire the capacity to recognize exemplifying instances.[11]

But Hick's account does not show that belief in God can reasonably be based on experience. The major problem here comes in its use of the notion of experiencing-as. Clearly there is a use for this idea, as the psychologists' pictures noted by Hick seem to show. Sometimes we find that something which undergoes no change first appears to us in one way and then in another. But can we regard all experience as experience-as? Hick says that we can, that just as one can see-as on some occasions so one can experience-as on all occasions. But if Hick is right it follows that when we experience something and when we characterize it on the basis of experience there is always in principle available an alternative experience and characterization, an alternative way of experiencing-as which is epistemically on a level with it. We experience something as an X, say, and therefore we call it an X. But we could in principle experience it as a Y and we could in principle characterize it as a Y. Surely, however, we must sometimes say that we experience things and that they are exactly as we say they are. If we cannot sometimes say this then how could we ever, as we often wish to do and as it often seems reasonable to do, seriously convict people of mistakenly identifying things? From the fact that someone experiences something as such and such it does not follow that he is right in what he says is there. One may often be able to say that something can be experienced either as this or as that; but one cannot always say this. On some occasions 'Here is an X' is either true or false. And on some occasions

'Here is a Y' is either true or false. And this point is presumably one that Hick must ultimately accept himself. For he seems clear enough that all experience really is experience-as. He seems clear, in other words, that his thesis about experience is correct.

So Hick's analysis still leaves us saying that even though people see things in one way they can be wrong. But that means that Hick's account leaves us with no particular reason for saying that people who claim to see the world as God's world are not just deluding themselves. They say that the world is God's world, but why can we not reply that they are unreasonable in saying so? Only, according to Hick, because all experience can be interpreted differently and everything can be seen either as this or as that, either as created by God or as not. But that position cannot cope with the fact that just because I experience X as Y it does not follow that I am reasonable in holding that it is Y. Just because some people see the world as God's world it does not follow that they are reasonable in saying that it is. Something other than the fact that they experience it as such seems to be required.

Where, then, does all this leave us on the question of experience and God? If my arguments have been correct it seems that though various objections can be made to the view that it is unreasonable to believe in God on the basis of experience, the whole notion of an experience of God either collapses into something that looks like the notion of being convinced by an argument or is just very difficult to understand. Experience of dogs and cats and people is one thing; but experience of what God is supposed to be seems quite different. It is far from clear that its nature can even be elucidated, let alone judged as something to which one could appeal as providing a reasonable ground for belief in God. This conclusion is independent of any reason, apart from experience, which we may have for believing in God, and, of course, there are evidently people who would disagree with it. Whether the reader is one of these is something he can now go on to consider for himself.

8 The attributes of God – 1 Eternity

We have already seen that people who believe in the Judaeo-Christian concept of God have more to say about God than that there is one. They ascribe certain attributes to God. These have often been the subject of lengthy philosophical debate and it now seems appropriate to say something more about them than has so far been said in earlier chapters. It will not be possible to discuss all the attributes that have been ascribed to God within Judaeo-Christianity, but we can say something about some of the most important. The ones I have chosen to talk about are eternity and omniscience. The first will concern us in this chapter, the second in Chapter 9. The question that basically confronts us throughout is simply this: is it reasonable to suppose that there is a God with these attributes?

The meaning of divine eternity

The notion of divine eternity is especially difficult to discuss since it has been understood in two distinct senses. For some people divine eternity means timelessness; others, however, have urged that God is only eternal in the sense that he is without beginning or end.

Theologically speaking it is the notion of eternity as timelessness that has had the greatest influence. It can be found in writers like Anselm, Augustine of Hippo (354–430), Aquinas, John Calvin (1509–64), and Friedrich Schleiermacher (1768–1834). Perhaps its most famous exponent is Boethius (c.480–524), whose definition of eternity as timelessness has become classic. Eternity, says Boethius, 'is the complete, simultaneous and perfect possession of everlasting life' (*aeternitas est interminabilis vitae tota simul et perfecta possessio*).[1]

The claim that God is timeless involves two assertions. The first is that God has no temporal extension, i.e. that he has no duration. As Augustine puts it: 'Thy years do not come and go; while these years of ours do come and go, in order that they might come. . . . Thy present day does not give place to tomorrow, nor indeed, does it take the place of yesterday. Thy present day is eternity.'[2] Second, to say that God is timeless is to assert that God has no temporal location, i.e. that there is no 'before' and 'after' with him. As St. Anselm declares: 'So it is not that you existed yesterday, or will exist tomorrow, but that yesterday, today and tomorrow, you simply are. Or rather, you exist neither yesterday, today, nor tomorrow, but you exist directly right outside time.'[3]

This view of divine eternity is an exceedingly difficult one to grasp; but the second view is less demanding, at least at first glance. Here the idea is simply that God just goes on and on, that nothing brought him into existence and that there is no time in the future when he will cease to be. In his book *The Coherence of Theism* Swinburne adopts this understanding of divine eternity:

If a creator of the universe exists now, he must have existed at least as long as there have been other logically contingent existing things. . . . However, traditionally theists believe not merely that this spirit, God, exists now or has existed as long as created things, but that he is an eternal being. This seems to mean, firstly, that he has always existed – that there was no time at which he did not exist. . . . Let us put this point by saying that they believe that he is backwardly eternal. The supposition that a spirit of the above kind is backwardly eternal seems to be a coherent one. . . . The doctrine that God is eternal seems to involve, secondly, the doctrine that the above spirit will go on existing for ever. . . . I will put this point by saying that he is forwardly eternal. This too seems to be a coherent suggestion.[4]

Objections to a timeless God

Since most of the controversy about God's eternity has begun with the notion of eternity as timelessness, perhaps we had better plunge into the deep end immediately and consider whether it is reasonable to talk in terms of a timeless God. A number of arguments have been advanced to the effect that it is not. At this stage I simply present them without comment.

One argument is concerned with the notions of coherence and conceivability. According to some people one cannot talk reasonably about a timeless God since the whole notion of timeless existence is incoherent or unintelligible. For one thing, we can have no idea of what such existence would be like. Secondly, if anything exists at all, it must exist at some time, for to exist at all is to exist at some time.

This argument is sometimes related to another. According to this one God cannot reasonably be said to be timeless since other things must be said of him, always assuming that he exists at all, and these other things are incompatible with his being timeless. In other words, the idea here is that the notion of a timeless God would render theism internally contradictory.

But what is it that critics find incompatible with God's timelessness?

Three things mainly: God's personal perfection, God's ability to act, and God's knowledge.

The view that God's personal perfection rules out his timelessness has been particularly popular in the twentieth century largely as a result of the work of a group of theologians called Process Theologians, of whom an eminent representative is Charles Hartshorne.[5] According to Hartshorne we regard people as fully personal if they are capable of love and if they are both passive, and thereby responsive to their environment, as well as active, and thereby able to take initiatives. In that case, however, God's personal perfection requires that he be able to love and that he be both passive and active. God must therefore sympathize with his creatures and be affected by what goes on in the world. Thus God undergoes joys and sorrows and his knowledge undergoes development. In short, God changes. But if God changes he cannot be timeless since a timeless being cannot really change in itself.

The point about God's ability to act is a conceptual one. The idea here is that if God acts then he must be in time since to act at all logically depends on acting at some time. Thus Swinburne says that 'If we say that P brings about X, we can always sensibly ask *when* does he bring it about? If we say that P punishes Q, we can always sensibly ask *when* does he punish Q. . . . If P at t brings about X, then necessarily X comes into existence (simultaneously with or) subsequently to P's action. . . . And so on.'[6]

Finally, the argument about God's knowledge is simply that if, as is commonly said, God is knowledgeable, if, indeed, he is omniscient, then he must know things now and he must have known them in the past. Furthermore, he must know them when they come about in the future. But all this must mean that he exists in time. Thus Anthony Kenny argues that if God is timeless then his knowledge is extremely restricted. 'It seems', he says, 'an extraordinary way of affirming God's omniscience if a person, when asked what God knows *now*, must say "Nothing", and when asked what he knew *yesterday*, must again say "Nothing", and must yet again say "Nothing" when asked what God will know *tomorrow*.'[7]

A final line of argument sometimes advanced against the reasonableness of belief in a timeless God is one based on Scripture. The argument is simply that in Scripture the eternity of God is eternity in the sense of endless duration.

Are the objections conclusive?

In considering the merits of the above objections we can begin with the one about coherence and intelligibility. And perhaps the first thing to say is that it is obviously expressing an evident truth. We can put it by saying that if 'intelligible' means 'understandable', 'conceivable', 'imaginable', or something like that, then the reality referred to in talking of timeless existence is not intelligible. It seems very hard indeed to conjure up any picture of timeless existence. It might be said that we are already familiar with things that exist timelessly. What about numbers and logical truths? But whether and how these can be said to exist is a difficult philosophical problem. Nor does it seem particularly relevant to the question of God's timelessness. For whatever else may be true of numbers and logical truths, it surely cannot be that they exercise anything like the causality commonly ascribed to God. As far as theists are concerned, God is operative; and it is just here that the problem of intelligibility begins to bite. Whenever we think of things operating, whenever we think of things with causal power, we seem to be thinking of things existing in time. We are thinking of things like men pushing pens and acids burning through substances.

But it is one thing to say this and another to say that timeless existence is not intelligible in the strong sense that it is flatly impossible, or, as the first of our objections put it, incoherent. And a case can be made for denying this second and stronger contention.

It will help at this stage if the reader thinks back to some remarks made earlier. I have already pointed out that one way of deciding whether something could be so is to see whether there is any reason for thinking that it is so. Now someone who says that the notion of timeless existence is flatly impossible or incoherent means that there could not be timeless existence. But there is reason for saying that there is.

Referring back to the argument of Chapter 5, it is, I suggest, reasonable to believe in a cause of all existing things; a cause, furthermore, which cannot be regarded as a particular thing over and against the many things that exist. If this is so, then there is timeless existence. Why? Because (*a*) the cause of all things cannot be said to change or even to be capable of changing, and (*b*) only what can be said to change or to be capable of changing can be in time. The defence of (*a*) is that if X can or does change, then X must be some particular thing, but the cause of all existing things cannot be such. The defence of (*b*) is that if X does not or cannot change, then no temporal predicates can intelligibly be ascribed to it. That is why we are tempted (if we are tempted) to say that numbers and logical truths are timeless. They are what they are in total independence of changes occurring in the universe. Nothing that happens is going to affect the number 9, and nothing that happens is going to alter the fact that nothing can be simultaneously perfectly square and perfectly round. The connection between time and change is also what leads writers like Hartshorne to deny that God is timeless. They want to ascribe change to God and this would seem to put him in time; he would *first* be like this and *then* be like that.

I suggest, then, that the notion of timeless existence is a coherent one and that sense can be given to it with reference to the cosmological argument, though it also seems that such existence is unimaginable. But what of the objections to the notion of a timeless God based on positions like those of Hartshorne, Swinburne, and Kenny?

Hartshorne's position has a number of advantages from the viewpoint of someone who wishes to believe in God. One of these lies in the fact that it understands God's eternity in terms of endless duration and can thereby be related to the dominant biblical way of talking about divine eternity. In other words, the last of the objections to a timeless God noted in the preceding section seems correct as a statement of fact. As John L. McKenzie shows, 'The philosophical concept of eternity is not clearly expressed in either the O.T. or N.T. The Hb. 'olam and the Gk. aiōn both signify primarily an indefinitely extended period of time beyond the lifetime of a single person.'[8] In his article on aiōn/aiōnios in Kittel's *Theological Dictionary of the New Testament*[9] Sasse sums up the New Testament position thus:

The unending eternity of God and the time of the world, which is limited by its creation and conclusion, are contrasted with one another. Eternity is thought of as unending time – for how else can human thought picture it? – and the eternal being of God is represented as pre-existence and post-existence. . . . The NT took over the OT and Jewish view of divine eternity along with the ancient formulae. There was new development, however, to the extent that the statements concerning God's eternity were extended to Christ.

But whatever may be the biblical way of talking (and, as Sasse himself indicates, it need only be a way of talking), there are serious objections to Hartshorne's position. The major one should now be clear in the light of what I have already been arguing. For if it is said that God is the cause of the existence of all things then God cannot change and must be timeless.

Hartshorne, of course, may reply that if that is the case then he is not interested in God and prefers to stick with his timeful, personal deity. But if the argument of Chapters 5 and 6 is correct this move is open to an obvious objection. As Hartshorne sees it, God is involved in a social context just like men and women; in this sense his God is personal, and that is why he wants to speak of him experiencing joy and sorrow. According to Hartshorne, just as I can feel joy and sorrow at things, so can God. But if that is true then Hartshorne's God is just as much part of the world of existing and ordered things as men and women are, and it is therefore reasonable to hold that he is caused to exist by a source of existing things.

In other words, the existence of Hartshorne's God raises the question of something beyond it. His God cannot be ultimate in the way that those who believe in God normally maintain that he is. Instead he is very much a being among beings. Nor, of course, is his future at all secure. Given that God is as Hartshorne describes him, it seems reasonable to regard his existence as dependent on a cause other than himself. But what guarantee does he have that this cause will not cease to bring it about that he exists? Here, at least, the notion of a timeless God has an advantage over that of a temporal one. Those who believe in God have regularly wanted to ascribe to him a kind of permanence or independence which will enable them to be confident that he will not cease to exist. But, clearly, if God is timeless then the idea of his ceasing to exist makes no sense. If X ceases to exist then it must be true that there was a time before this event when X existed, and X must therefore have existed at some time.

So much, then, for Hartshorne. But what of Swinburne's point about divine action? With reference to it one can again, I think, argue that we do not have good grounds for holding that talk about a timeless God is unreasonable.

At first glance what Swinburne says seems clearly true. That is to say, it is tempting to agree that:

1. If P brings about X we can ask 'When does he bring it about?'
2. If someone says that P punishes Y then it makes sense to ask when he does so.
3. If P at t brings about X then X comes into existence simultaneously with or subsequently to P's action.

But how do we know that 1–3 are always true? Swinburne, as far as I can see, just assumes that they must be, that they express logically necessary truths. And as long as we keep our mind fixed on their use of the variable letter P it is tempting to agree. But in a discussion of timelessness and God, P = God. And it is far from clear that 1–3 are logically true when God is their subject. For if there could be a God who is timeless then obviously they are not necessarily true. But, as we have seen, if God is taken to be the cause of existing things he must be timeless. Therefore they are not necessarily true. And the inference to make from this is that when, for example, God is said to bring things about then 'bring about' has a sense appropriate to its subject, God, a sense which does not allow us to be bound by the stipulations involved in arguments like the present one of Swinburne.

A possible reply to this line of thinking would be to say that if, for example, 'brings about' does not mean 'brings about at some time' then it means nothing at all. But I have already indicated why this need not be so. For, clearly, 'brings about' means 'causes', and if God can be both timeless and the cause of existing things then God can bring things about without being at some time in bringing them about. He cannot, of course, arrange that things in time brought about by him are brought about at no time. And this, perhaps, is partly what Swinburne is getting at. But the temporal reference here is wholly on the side of the things of which 'is brought about' is truly predicated. It is not necessarily on the side of what brings them about, and if what I have been arguing about God is correct, and if it is God who is said to bring these things about, then it could not be. In other words, if it is coherent to suppose that there is a timeless cause of existing things it is coherent to suppose (1) that things can be said to be brought about by God, (2) that these things can be brought about at some time, but (3) that God does not have to exist at some time to bring it about that 'brought about at some time' is true of whatever is brought about by God. To put it another way, we can certainly ask when something was brought about, but it is not logically necessary that what brings it about is itself something in time. This is because it is coherent to talk of a timeless cause of existing things.

It is also, I think, coherent to say that if X is timeless then X can still be knowledgeable. The topic of divine omniscience will properly concern us in the next chapter so I do not wish to argue here that the notion of omniscience is intrinsically coherent. But it is relevant at this point to consider the suggestion that there is a contradiction in holding that X can be knowledgeable if X is timeless, i.e. that knowing is inevitably only open to something in time.

Why should one say that if X knows something then X knows it at some time? The obvious reply is that it is normally people, and sometimes animals, who are said to know things, and since people and animals exist in time (as far as we understand them) then that they know something is either true at some time or not true at all. But just as it does not follow that if X brings Y about then X is in time, so it does not follow that if X knows something then X knows it at some time, though it may perhaps be that X can know timelessly something that is the case at some time. In seeing why this is so we must go back to the point about denying that some statement is logically possible because one has reason to think that what it asserts is actually true. And with reference to this point we also need to return to the conclusions arrived at in Chapter 6. As we saw, it seems reasonable to hold that there is an intelligent cause of the order in the universe, a cause which can also be said to be the cause of the existence of things. Now, while there seems no necessary connection between the notions 'being a cause' and 'being knowledgeable' (as I suggested in Chapter 5), there is such a connection between 'being intelligent' and 'being knowledgeable'; i.e. if X is intelligent then X is knowledgeable (except perhaps when X is the subject in statements like 'The most intelligent arrangement won the competition', which introduce a use of 'intelligent' not relevant to the present discussion – obviously a design is not know-ledgeable, but nor is it intelligent in any other way than by showing that its designer is intelligent). Now, if this is so, it seems that if it is reasonable to say that there is an intelligent cause of the existence of things then it is reasonable to say that this cause is knowledgeable. Yet we have already seen that the cause of the existence of things can reasonably be regarded as timeless. The cause of the existence of things must therefore be both knowledgeable and timeless, in which case it is wrong to say that being knowledgeable and being timeless are logically incompatible. This in turn entails that a timeless God could yet be said to be knowledgeable.

At this stage, in the discussion, then, the position seems to be this: (1) It is coherent to suppose that there is timeless existence. (2) The notion of a changing, timeful God is open to objection. (3) It is coherent to suppose that things are brought about by what is timeless and knowledgeable. This means, I think, that the objections to a timeless God are answerable and that there is positive reason for saying that God is timeless. Thus there is positive reason for holding that God is eternal in the classical theistic sense of being timeless.

But it is, perhaps, worth adding one point. Suppose one opts for the view that God is eternal in the sense of existing for ever. And suppose an objector retorts that this is a nonsensical view since nothing can be con-ceived of as existing for ever. Would this mean that the endless-duration view of divine eternity entailed that there could not be a God? It has been strongly argued that it would not. Swinburne, for instance, suggests that if it is coherent to suppose that God exists at the present time then it is 'coherent to suppose that he exists at any other nameable time; and, if that is coherent, then surely it is coherent to suppose that there exists a being now such that however far back in time you count years you do not reach the beginning of its existence.'[10] He continues: 'We, perhaps, cease to exist at death. But we can surely conceive of a being now existent such that whatever future nameable time you choose, he has not by that time ceased to exist. . . . A being who is both backwardly and forwardly eternal we may term an eternal being.'[11]   I am inclined to agree with Swinburne here, so perhaps the notion of eternity as continuous existence is not demonstrably meaningless. But whether it makes any sense to suppose that God could have eternity in this sense is another matter. So much depends on one's reaction to the view that God is timeless.

9 The attributes of God –
2 Omniscience

Continuing with the theme of divine attributes, we come now to the topic of divine omniscience. As with the view that God is eternal, we can begin by asking the obvious question about what is supposed to be at stake. To start with, then, what does it mean to say that God is omniscient?

The meaning of divine omniscience

It would be generally agreed that 'omniscient' means 'all-knowing' and that to call God omniscient is to say that he is all-knowing. But those who have called God omniscient have had different views about what it means for God to be all-knowing. On one point they are agreed: they agree that God's omniscience is a matter of his knowing what is true and what is not true. But what this amounts to is a matter of debate among them and at least two schools of thought can be distinguished.

The first depends on the view that God is timeless. It holds that what God knows is all that was true, is true, and will be true. And it adds that God knows all this timelessly. According to this view of omniscience, therefore, 'God is omniscient' means that God timelessly knows all that was, is, and will be true.

The second approach to omniscience presupposes that God is not timeless. It therefore holds that the knowing referred to in 'God is all-knowing' is something that is the case at some time, the time in question being that at which it is said that God is all-knowing. But within this second approach it is possible to distinguish different views about what God knows. First, it is said that God knows all that was, is, and will be true. On this account, to say that God is omniscient is to say that he knows all this now. Second, it is said that God knows all that was and is true, but he only knows what will be true if this is determined by something that is presently the case. The point of this amendment is to prevent God from knowing now what people will freely do in the future. Behind it lies the assumption that a free action cannot be determined by past states.

We have, then, three distinct understandings of 'God is omniscient':

1. God timelessly knows all that was, is, and will be true.
2. God now knows all that was, is, and will be true.
3. God now knows only what was and is true, and all that will be true in so far as it is determined by what is already the case.

Objections to divine omniscience

A number of objections have been raised against the view that it is reasonable to believe in an omniscient God. Some of these involve claims that we have already encountered, e.g. that the notion of a timeless God is incoherent. This view has recently been defended by Norman Kretzmann.[1] He notes that there are a number of statements whose truth value changes consider for himself how they might be applied to the notion of an omniscient God and what might be said about their general cogency. What concerns us now are objections to the notion of an omniscient God which focus specifically on the idea of omniscience. And here two in particular deserve to be noted.

According to the first, the notion of omniscience is internally incoherent. This view has recently been defended by Norman Kretzmann.[1] He notes that there are a number of statements whose truth value changes through the passing of time. If someone were to say 'It is now 4 o'clock' at 4 o'clock they would be uttering a true statement. At 5 o'clock, however, the statement would be false. Now, says Kretzmann, consider the claim that God is omniscient. This claim must mean that God knows all there is to be known and that God knows the truth of statements like 'It is now 4 o'clock.' But while it is possible to know that such statements are true one cannot always know that they are true, for sometimes they are not. Thus at time t2 God cannot know what Jones knew at t1 when Jones knew that it was then 4 o'clock. And therefore God cannot be omniscient.

The second objection to the notion of omniscience is a very famous one. It hinges on the view that if God is omniscient then human freedom is impossible. As most commonly presented the argument runs thus:

1. If God is omniscient he knows all that will be true in the future.
2. If someone knows that-P it follows that-P.
3. If God knows that some future event will come to pass it cannot be true that the event will not come to pass.
4. If it is true that some future event cannot but come to pass then the event is necessary.
5. If a human action is free it cannot be necessary.
6. Therefore, if God is omniscient there can be no future, free human actions.

This argument is affirming a dilemma for belief in an omniscient God. People who believe in God normally want to say that human beings can perform future, free actions. But if God is omniscient can there be any such actions?

Comments on the objections to divine omniscience

Is Kretzmann's argument against the coherence of omniscience a successful one? One might be tempted to reply to it by saying tha. God can know what Jones knew at t1 when Jones knew it was then 4 o'clock since both God and Jones can know that at 4 o'clock it is 4 o'clock. But there is surely a difference between knowing at 4 o'clock that it is 4 o'clock and knowing that at 4 o'clock it is 4 o'clock. This point is brought out by Arthur Prior who asks us to contrast a timeless truth with one which is only true at some time. He takes the statement 'The 1960 final examinations at Manchester are now over', on which he comments:

It's true now, but it wasn't true a year ago . . . and so far as I can see all that can be said on this subject timelessly is that the finishing date of the 1960 final examinations is an earlier one than August 29th, and this is *not* the thing we know when we know that those exams are over . . . what we know when we know that the 1960 final examinations are over can't just be a timeless relation between dates because this isn't the thing we're *pleased* about when we're pleased that the exams are over.[2]

Having granted Prior's point, however, it can still be said that Kretzmann's argument is answerable. Even if it is true that God cannot know on Tuesday that it is Monday, why cannot he know what I know on Monday when I say (truly) 'I know that it is now Monday'?

Here it is worth noting some observations made against Kretzmann by Hector Neri Castañeda. He asks us to consider the following principle:

If a sentence of the form 'X knows that a person Y knows that . . .' formulates a true statement, the person X knows the statement formulated by the clause filling the blank '. . .'.[3]

This principle seems true. If you know that Oxford is in England, and if I know that you know this, presumably I know what you know. If Castañeda's principle is correct, however, then Kretzmann seems mistaken.

Suppose I know on June 1st that 'It is now June 1st' is true. Surely you can know on June 2nd that I knew what I did on June 1st. And you could report your knowledge by saying something like 'I know that he knew yesterday that it was then June 1st.' Thus you can know on June 2nd what I know on June 1st, though you will use different words from me in reporting what is known, and though anybody who reports your knowledge will use different words from me in doing the same. In that case, however, it would now seem that even though God cannot, for example, know at 5 o'clock that 'It is now 4 o'clock' is true he can, for all Kretzmann has shown, know that 'It is now 4 o'clock' was known at 4 o'clock to be true, which is the same as knowing what is known when it is known at 4 o'clock that 'It is now 4 o'clock' is true.

But all of this does nothing to show that if God is omniscient there can still be free actions. But is it really true that if God is omniscient, there cannot be free actions?

Let us consider an example. Suppose I now suggest to you that you have read more about the philosophy of religion than is good for you and that when you have read to the end of this sentence you should put this book down and do something useful. Assuming that you have ignored my perfectly sound advice, ask yourself whether or not you can now bring it about that you put down this book after reading the last sentence. Obviously, the answer is no. You can put the book down after this sentence. And you can put it down after this one. But you cannot do anything about the fact that you did not put it down after that one. And if you are still reading I am afraid that you are now stuck in the same way with five more sentences.

What this example shows is that there is a sort of inevitability about the past. Given that something has happened, then there is nothing we can do to bring it about that it has not happened. But suppose what has happened is that somebody came to know something about the future. It seems that his knowing is also something fixed or unalterable. Yet to say that Brown knows that-P is to say that-P is true. Brown can hope, believe, guess, surmise, or fear that he is an idiot. But if Brown knows that he is an idiot, then he is an idiot. If, then, Brown knows on Monday that it will rain on Tuesday, then evidently it will rain on Tuesday. But if Brown knew on Monday that it would rain, and if the past is unalterable, then it seems that Tuesday's rain was unalterable as soon as Brown knew about it on Monday. In the same way, it seems that if Brown knew on Monday that Jones would take an overdose on Tuesday, then Jones's overdose was unpreventable on Monday when Brown knew about it. And, to get back to God again, it seems that if God knows at time 1 that somebody will do something at time 2 then the person is bound to do it. For God's knowing at time 1 what the person will do at time 2 is unalterable by time 2 and it seems to entail that he will do it.

But although this may seem a strong argument against the reasonableness of believing in an omniscient God, it cannot be taken to show that belief in such a God is unreasonable. For the simple fact is that if God knows at time 1 that P will freely do X at time 2 then what God knows is that P will freely do X. In other words, if God knows at time 1 that P will freely do X at time 2 then God's knowledge at time 1 is dependent on P freely doing X at time 2. Given that at time 1 God knows that P will freely do X at time 2, it may be unalterable after time 1 that P will freely do X. But the unalterable fact at time 1 just could not be at all if P were not free to do X at time 2. For if P were not free at time 2, then God could not know at time 1 that P would be free at time 2.

The thrust of this argument seems to have been realized by Aquinas, whose own discussion of divine knowledge and human freedom is worth noting at this point. He observes:

'All that God knows must necessarily be', is usually distinguished: it can apply either to the thing or to the statement. Understood of the thing, the proposition is taken independently of the fact of God's knowing, and false, giving the sense 'Every thing that God knows is a necessary thing'. Or it can be understood of the statement, and thus it is taken in conjunction with the fact of God's knowing, and true, giving the sense, 'The statement, *a thing known by God is*, is necessary.'[4]

The question at issue is whether future, free actions are possible given that God knows them in advance. If a future action is not free, it might be said to be necessary. But when dealing with necessity we need to distinguish between what philosophers have referred to as necessity *de dicto* and necessity *de re*. We would be dealing with necessity *de dicto* if we were dealing with a proposition that is logically true, e.g. 'If Socrates is sitting, he is sitting.' We would be dealing with necessity *de re* if, by contrast, we had a statement like 'Socrates is sitting necessarily.' This is a statement about Socrates, and it says that nothing could, as a matter of fact, prevent Socrates from sitting. With this distinction in mind we can see what Aquinas is saying. Someone who thinks that 'God is omniscient' and 'There are some future, free actions' are incompatible wants us to accept that if God is omniscient, then future, free actions are necessary. But this could mean either (1) ' "If God knows that Socrates will sit tomorrow, then Socrates will sit tomorrow" is necessarily true', or (2) ' "God knows that Socrates will sit tomorrow" entails that Socrates will necessarily sit tomorrow.' Now (1) is true, but (2) is not. There is no contradiction in the supposition that Socrates is not always sitting as a matter of necessity. 'If Socrates is sitting, he is sitting' is necessary; but this does not show that Socrates always sits necessarily, that nothing can stop Socrates sitting, that 'sitting' is part of the meaning of 'Socrates'.

So there is no contradiction in holding that God can know of a free action in advance. And this is one reason why there is no contradiction between divine omniscience and human freedom. But another reason can be given for denying such a contradiction.

In discussing the argument about omniscience and freedom I have so far accepted what is obviously one of its crucial premises, viz. that divine omniscience involves foreknowledge. As we have seen, on some accounts of omniscience this is true. But it is obviously not true for the view that 'God is omniscient' means that God timelessly knows all that was, is, and will be true. For on this view of omniscience there can be no divine foreknowledge and therefore there cannot be a problem about reconciling belief in God's foreknowledge and belief in human freedom. In other words, the problem we have just been considering leaves quite untouched the view that God's omniscience is timeless.

An omniscient God?

But does all this mean that it is reasonable to believe in an omniscient God? By itself, of course, it does not. Yet if the arguments of the last chapter are acceptable, it seems that if God is taken to be the cause of all existing things, then he is both timeless and knowledgeable. Might it not therefore be argued that it is reasonable to believe in an omniscient God? I think that the answer to this question is affirmative, given that 'omniscient' bears the sense 'timelessly knows all that was, is, and will be true'. But in order to see why, we need to pause to consider what would be involved in knowing all that was, is, and will be true. And the question that needs to be asked here is 'What can be known?'

In introducing this question I am not trying to initiate a discussion of the scope of knowledge. That would obviously be impracticable here. The question at issue now is 'What must be true of X if X can be known?'

Since one cannot know what is unintelligible, part of the answer must be that if X can be known then X is intelligible. But what can this mean? Various answers are, perhaps, possible, but if X is intelligible then X must certainly be identifiable and characterizable. If X cannot be identified or characterized in any way then X is unintelligible in the strongest possible sense.

Suppose, now, we ask what X must be like if it is identifiable and characterizable. Again it might be possible to offer various answers. But if X is identifiable and characterizable, then X must surely possess some degree of order. For if X cannot be spoken of as continuing to be what it is, then X cannot be identified or characterized at all. And if X can be spoken of as continuing to be what it is, then X is somehow ordered.

If X can be known, then, X must possess some degree of order. But what has all this to do with divine omniscience? At this point we can go back to what has already been argued in earlier chapters.

In Chapter 6 I argued that it is reasonable to account for order in terms of an intelligent and knowledgeable cause of order. Now as far as I can see, this must mean that whatever causes order can reasonably be said to know whatever is orderly, since it is with reference to the fact that order is order that knowledge can be ascribed to its cause. But I have also argued that the intelligent cause of order can be identified with the cause of the existence of things, and in Chapter 7 we saw reason for adding that such a cause can reasonably be regarded as timelsss. So it seems that the existence of orderly things can be reasonably accounted for in terms of a timeless, intelligent cause that can be said to know order by being its cause. But if what I have been arguing above is correct, then nothing can be known unless it possesses some kind of order, which means that all knowable things possess some degree of order. If, however, the existence of orderly things can be accounted for in terms of a timeless intelligent cause that can be said to know order by being its cause, it follows that all knowable things are known by a timeless intelligent cause of their existence. Since this cause is the cause of anything that possesses order, it is the cause of all that ever did possess order, all that now possesses order, and all that will possess order. Since it is timeless and since it knows what possesses order, it knows all that ever did possess order, all that now possesses order, and all that will possess order. But its knowledge cannot exist at some time. Given, now, that an omniscient God can be regarded as a timeless knower of all that was, is, and will be, it follows that it is reasonable to hold that there is such a God.

In other words, it seems that (1) given the equation 'knowable thing = ordered thing' and (2) given that order is reasonably accounted for with reference to a timeless cause of the existence of orderly things, a cause that knows all orderly things, then whatever is knowable at any time is timelessly known by this cause. And given that this cause can be regarded as God, it follows that it is reasonable to believe in an omniscient God whose omniscience consists in his timelessly knowing all that was, is, and will be. For this reason I suggest that belief in an omniscient God is reasonable. This conclusion depends, of course, on earlier arguments that I have offered. Before accepting it the reader will naturally have to satisfy himself that these actually work.

10 Morality and religion

We have so far considered a number of questions relevant to the central Judaeo-Christian belief that there is a God. But it is now time to proceed to some other topics to which philosophers of religion have paid attention. The first is that of morality and religion. In this book it is impossible to do justice to all the issues involved so I shall confine myself to considering one major question commonly raised by philosophers: is there a relationship between morality and religion?

Views on the relationship between morality and religion

Let us begin to consider this question by noting some of the answers that have been given to it. In fact, a number of different ones can be distinguished. Broadly speaking, however, most of these can be sorted out into one of three kinds. These hold respectively (1) that morality somehow supports religion, (2) that morality is somehow included in religion, (3) that morality and religion are opposed to each other.

(1) Morality as support for religion

Those who take the view that morality supports religion usually argue that there is something about morality that makes it reasonable to believe in God. A good example of a writer who thinks in these terms is Kant. As we have seen, Kant has little time for the ontological argument for God's existence. But he does not therefore conclude that belief in God is irrational. On the contrary, he argues that morality points towards God.

In Kant's view a number of factors go to make up morality. These include moral obligation and the freedom to act in accordance with this. Kant also thinks that there is an obligation to bring about the absolutely perfect state of affairs, which he calls the *summum bonum*. In this state of affairs virtue prevails along with the crowning of virtue with happiness, and, for Kant, morality demands the realization of the *summum bonum*. But this is manifestly not realized in this life. Even though people can be totally dedicated morally speaking, factors beyond their control prevent them from realizing it. According to Kant, there must therefore be something other than man which can ensure that the absolutely perfect state of affairs is realized.

We ought to endeavour to promote the *summum bonum*, which, therefore, must be possible. Accordingly, the existence of a cause of all nature, distinct from nature itself, and containing the principle of this connection, namely, of the exact harmony of happiness with morality, is also *postulated*. . . . Therefore, the *summum bonum* is possible in the world only on the supposition of a Supreme Being having a causality corresponding to moral character. . . . Now it was seen to be a duty for us to promote the *summum bonum*; consequently it is not merely allowable, but it is a necessity connected with duty as a requisite, that we should presuppose the possibility of this *summum bonum*; and this is possible only on the condition of the existence of God, it inseparably connects the supposition of this with duty; that is it is morally necessary to assume the existence of God.[1]

As Kant sees it, then, the fact that morality demands the realization of the *summum bonum*, and the fact that only God can see to it that the *summum bonum* comes about, lead to the conclusion that there is a God. But this argument is not the only one that has been offered in defence of the view that morality gives us grounds for belief in God. Many writers have argued that one can infer the existence of God from the existence of moral commands or laws. This, it is said, implies the existence of a moral lawgiver or a moral commander. Thus H. P. Owen writes: 'It is impossible to think of a command without also thinking of a command*er*. . . . A clear choice faces us. Either we take moral claims to be self-explanatory modes of *im*personal existence or we explain them in terms of a personal God.'[2] To arguments like this there has often been added a reference to responsibility and guilt. People often feel morally responsible and they often feel guilty if they fail to do their moral duty. But, so the argument goes, this situation makes no real sense unless moral laws have a personal explanation. In fact, it is argued, moral laws inspire guilt and responsibility because they have a personal basis in the personal will of God. Thus John Henry Newman (1801–90) writes: 'If, as is the case, we feel responsibility, are ashamed, are frightened, at transgressing the voice of conscience, this implies that there is One to whom we are responsible, before whom we are ashamed, whose claim upon us we fear.'[3]

A variation on this position has been developed to great effect by Illtyd Trethowan.[4] Trethowan eschews talk about a moral *argument* for God's existence since he thinks that one can come to know of God by virtue of a direct awareness or apprehension. But this must be mediated in some way; it is not, so to speak, a matter of meeting God face to face. And, according to Trethowan, we are directly aware of God in our moral experience. In this, he says, we are confronted by absolute moral obligations and by absolute value; we are confronted, in fact, by God: 'The notion of value is bound up with the notion of obligation. To say that people are worth while, that they have value in themselves, is to say that there is something about them which makes a demand upon us, that we *ought* to make them part of our own project, identify ourselves with them in some sort. . . . I propose to say that an awareness of obligation is an awareness of God.'[5]

(2) *Morality as included in religion*

So much, then, for the view that morality supports religion. But what of the view that morality is included in religion? The basic idea here is that being moral is part of what being religious means.

One expression of it asserts that a morally obligatory action means 'an action that is willed by God'. On this account, from 'God wills me to do X' one can infer 'I am morally obliged to do X.' But this view can itself be broken up into at least two distinct positions. One can appreciate the difference involved by first considering an example.

Suppose someone joins an organization where there is a leader who issues orders. The leader says, 'You ought to do X', and everybody agrees with him. But suppose our new member says 'Yes, I ought to do X, but not because the leader tells me to. He is right in what he says, but the fact that he says it does not make it right.'

Now one version of the view we are at present concerned with is rather like the view of the new member in the above example. It holds that God always wills what is morally obligatory, but the mere fact of God's willing it does not by itself make anything morally obligatory. On this view, then, the moral value of an action can be deduced from the fact that God wills it, but an action is not morally obligatory just because God wills it.

According to the other version of the present view, however, this is not the case. On this version an action is established as morally obligatory by virtue of being willed by God. On this account whatever God wills is the morally right thing to do just because God wills it. People who defend this account sometimes argue that if one thinks that there are moral reasons that oblige one to refuse to do what God wills, then one has not understood what morality is all about. On their view there is no moral standard against which God's will can be judged. On the contrary, God's will creates moral standards.

So according to some theories morality is included in religion since being moral is doing what God wills. But other ways of including morality in religion have been suggested. A particularly famous one is defended in a much discussed lecture of R. B. Braithwaite. He writes:

My contention then is that the primary use of religious assertions is to announce allegiance to a set of moral principles.... A religious assertion, for me, is the assertion of an intention to carry out a certain behaviour policy, subsumable under a sufficiently general principle to be a moral one, together with the implicit or explicit statement, but not the assertion, of certain stories [see p.102].... A moral belief is an intention to behave in a certain way (a moral belief) together with the entertainment of certain stories associated with the intention in the mind of the believer.[6]

(3)   *Morality as opposed to religion*

All the above views take the line that there is no real disagreement between a moral point of view and a religious one. But according to some people this is mistaken. Both philosophical and theological writers can be brought in to illustrate this way of thinking.

The philosophical writers have largely been opposed to religion on moral grounds. An example is James Rachels. He says that belief in God involves a total and unqualified commitment to obey God's commands and that such commitment is not appropriate for a moral agent since 'to be a moral agent is to be an autonomous or self-directed agent.... The virtuous man is therefore identified with the man of integrity, i.e. the man who acts according to precepts which he can, on reflection, conscientiously approve in his own heart.'[7] Rachels therefore holds that one can disprove God's existence. He argues:

1. If any being is God, he must be a fitting object of worship.

2. No being could possibly be a fitting object of worship since worship requires the abandonment of one's role as an autonomous moral agent.

3. Therefore, there cannot be any being who is God.

Other philosophers, however, have argued differently for the view that morality is opposed to religion. Some have said that religious people can fail to make good citizens.[8] Others have pointed out that much evil has been brought about solely by religious people and their beliefs. One thinks here of the famous remark of Lucretius (99/94–55/51 BC): *Tantum religio potuit suadere malorum* – 'Such evil deeds could religion provoke.'[9] A similar sentiment can be found in the writings of Bertrand Russell. 'Religion', says Russell, 'prevents our children from having a rational education; religion prevents us from removing the fundamental causes of war; religion prevents us from teaching the ethic of scientific co-operation in place of the old fierce doctrines of sin and punishment. It is possible that mankind is on the threshold of a golden age; but if so, it will be necessary first to slay the dragon that guards the door, and this dragon is religion.'[10]

As I said above, theologians have also argued for a distinction between morality and religion. Take, for example, the Danish writer Søren Kierkegaard (1813–55). In *Fear and Trembling* he considers the biblical story of Abraham being told by God to sacrifice Isaac (Genesis 22). He says that Abraham was bound to do what God commanded. 'Here', he adds, 'there can be no question of ethics in the sense of morality . . . ordinarily speaking, a temptation is something which tries to stop a man from doing his duty, but in this case it is ethics itself which tries to prevent him from doing God's will. But what then is duty? Duty is quite simply the expression of the will of God.'[11] In this connection Kierkegaard talks about 'a teleological suspension of the ethical', an idea which can also be traced in the work of D. Z. Phillips, according to whom religious belief provides religious believers with their standard for evaluating actions. 'The religious concept of duty', writes Phillips, 'cannot be understood if it is treated as a moral concept. When the believer talks of doing his duty, what he refers to is doing the will of God. In making a decision, what is important for the believer is that it should be in accordance with the will of God. To a Christian, to do one's duty *is* to do the will of God. There is indeed no difficulty in envisaging the "ethical" as the obstacle to "duty" in this context.'[12]

Morality as grounds for belief in God

Let us now begin to consider the views just noted by turning first to the claim that one can move from morality to belief in God. Is the claim a reasonable one?

In some respects Kant's argument is rather impressive. It is widely accepted by philosophers that 'ought' implies 'can'. If I tell someone that they ought to do something it must surely be true that they can do it. It would be nonsense, for instance, to say to a polio victim 'You ought to walk to work.' One might therefore be tempted to argue that if the *summum bonum* ought to be realized then it can be realized. Since it cannot be realized by human agents one might therefore feel inclined to say that morality is absurd if God does not exist.

But Kant's argument is evidently mistaken. Even if we grant that the *summum bonum* ought to be realized, that it can be realized, and that man cannot ensure its realization, it still does not follow that only God can realize it. Why cannot the *summum bonum* be realized by something more powerful than man and less powerful than God? Why cannot a top-ranking angel do the job? Why not a pantheon of angels? Why not a pantheon of very clever and Kantian-minded angels?

A second difficulty with Kant's argument is that it is inconsistent. According to Kant the *summum bonum* is possible since man is under an obligation to realize it and since he can realize it. But Kant's argument for God hinges on the supposition that man cannot himself realize the *summum bonum*. Kant is therefore committed to the view that man can realize the *summum bonum* and to the view that he cannot.

So Kant's moral argument for God does not work. But what about such arguments as that moral laws imply a moral lawgiver and that the sense of moral responsibility and guilt implies the existence of God to whom we are responsible and before whom we feel guilty?

Anyone who proposes to answer this question must first know whether there is a moral law from which one might argue to a divine lawgiver. And whether there is such a law is a very big question which takes us straight into some of the most controversial areas of moral philosophy and which cannot be properly discussed in this book.[13] But we can note two major answers that have been given and the implications that these might be said to have.

To begin with, then, we can note that some philosophers believe in the existence of an objective moral law binding on all men. This law can be expressed in value judgements which are true independently of any human being's thoughts or attitudes. Men can come to know of it and they can either obey or disobey it.

According to other philosophers, however, there is no objective moral law. On this view it is not appropriate to speak of value judgements which are true independently of whatever people think or feel. On the contrary, so the argument goes, moral judgement is a subjective matter. According to some writers, it is the expression of emotion or the expression of some decision about behaviour. According to others, it is the product of man's desire to survive.

As I say, the rights and wrongs in this area cannot be gone into here. But suppose one adopts the first view. Does it follow that one can then reasonably infer the existence of God?

Here it seems to me that writers like Owen, while not having anything that could be regarded as a demonstrative case, yet have a plausible line of argument. They certainly hold to our first view about the moral law; they would say that there is an objective moral law. Yet it does seem odd, even though not self-contradictory, to grant this and to leave matters there. This point is well made by Trethowan. Writing from the viewpoint of one who endorses an objective view of morality, he says: 'The absoluteness of moral obligation, as I see it, is so far from being self-explanatory that if it were not made intelligible by being found in a metaphysical – and in fact, a theistic – context, I should be greatly tempted to hand it over to the anthropologists and the psychologists.'[14] This is not a watertight argument, but it does raise a problem for someone who believes in an objective and imperious moral law. If, furthermore, one already has reason for believing in God independently of moral considerations, one might well argue that there is some additional reason for thinking of the moral law with reference to God. For God is normally said to be purposive and intelligent. If one has reason to believe in God, one would thereby have available some model providing a context for talk about a non-human lawgiver.

But not everyone who has thought in terms of an objective moral law has interpreted it as pointing to a moral lawgiver, and it is now worth adding that belief in an objective moral law need not even suggest the existence of God. Owen seems to think that the moral law is analogous to laws promulgated by human beings. That is why he wants to talk about it with reference to a lawgiver. But others have held that though one can certainly make value judgements that are true independently of people's thoughts and feelings, these judgements gain their ultimate significance in terms of human wants and needs. On this account a moral judgement like 'P ought to do X' basically means something like 'If P does not want to lose out then P should do X.' Thus, for example, Peter Geach writes: 'One obviously relevant sort of reply to a question "Why shouldn't I?" is an appeal to something the questioner wants, and cannot get if he does so-and-so. I maintain that only such a reply is relevant and rational.'[15] And though this kind of view allows that a moral judgement can be absolutely true, though it is as objectivist a theory of moral judgement as one could desire, and though it accompanies talk about an objective moral law, it does not seem to imply that there is a God any more than the truth of an assertion like 'If you want to get to town by 3 o'clock then you need to catch the train at 2 o'clock.' It might be said that if one already has reason to believe in God independently of moral considerations, then the fact that there is a moral law in the present sense is only to be expected. One might argue, for example, that if there is a God who is intelligent and purposive then it is only to be expected that he would provide some objective standard against which people can decide whether or not some proposed course of action is likely to benefit them. But simply from the fact that there is such a standard there seems no particular reason for saying that there must be a God. One might, perhaps, argue that there could not be such a standard if people did not function in particular and predictable ways. And one might add that the fact that they do so function can be used as the premise of an argument for God's existence. But such an argument would be a version of the argument from design and would not depend for any of its strength on considerations deriving only from the notion of a moral law.

So the first of our views about the moral law can be seen as having conflicting interpretations. But the same cannot be said about the second.

For, quite clearly, if there is no objective, independent moral law there is no argument from a moral law to the existence of God as a moral lawgiver. And if moral judgements are just expressions of people's feelings or decisions and so on, it is hard to see that they can have any particular weight at all in an argument for God's existence. Not, at any rate, in an argument based on the moral law.

Is morality included in religion?

Let us now consider the claim that morality is included in religion either because God always wills what is morally obligatory or because 'action willed by God' is what 'morally obligatory action' means.

The first alternative evidently presupposes a number of things. For a start it presupposes that there are morally obligatory actions for God to will. Some people would deny that this is so, but suppose we let the presupposition pass. It would then seem that the view that morally obligatory actions are always willed by God depends on the truth of two assertions. The first is that there is a God who can be said to will things, who can be said to will morally obligatory actions, and whose will can be known. The second is that God always wills morally obligatory actions.

But is it reasonable to accept these assertions? Again I am afraid that we have come to a question that cannot be debated here for it raises a host of problems, many of which could occupy a volume to themselves. But one thing does seem fairly clear. Most people who believe in God believe that his will is totally perfect in that it is always directed to the production of what is good. If it is reasonable to believe in God, and if it is reasonable to believe this of him, then it is reasonable to believe that God does always will morally obligatory actions. For if there are such actions they are, by definition, directed towards producing what is good. And if God's will is always directed to the production of what is good, then he will always will such actions. If this point is accepted, it can be added that there is therefore no obvious absurdity in holding that morality is included in religion. For, as many people would see it, religion has to do with doing what God wills. If, then, God always wills what is morally obligatory, then simply by doing what is morally obligatory one will be doing what God wills.

Granted a fairly standard view of God, then, and granted that there is a God to correspond to it, it would be reasonable to hold that in one sense at least morality is included in religion. But what of the view that God's will determines what is morally obligatory? Many philosophers would regard it as totally unacceptable for several reasons. The two most often advanced are: (1) the view is morally unacceptable since it entails that if God willed some morally despicable action the action would thereby become a morally obligatory one; (2) the view assumes that from the fact that God wills some action it is possible to conclude that the action is morally obligatory. But from 'P wills X' one can never infer 'X is morally obligatory.'

How strong are these objections? A lot here depends on what view we are to take about certain moral judgements. When I was discussing the problem of evil in Chapter 3 I noted with regard to D. Z. Phillips and Richard Swinburne how two people could reach deadlock over certain moral questions. I also observed that it is hard to see how this deadlock can be resolved. Now in the present context some people would say that if one knew that God willed X, one could, depending on what X was, baldly declare that X is totally and unequivocally unacceptable from the moral point of view. These people would therefore say that (1) above is a legitimate conclusion which rules out the suggestion that God's will can be the deciding factor in saying what is and what is not morally obligatory. And in reply to this position I do not really see what can be said. If someone asserts that, for example, I am absolutely forbidden to kill innocent people, and if they add that this holds even if God wills that I kill some innocent people, then that person is evidently adopting a very fundamental moral position that could conceivably accommodate any argument brought against it.

But this does not mean that it is necessary to reject (1). For someone might say that accepting God's will as the ultimate moral criterion is itself a fundamental moral option. And if it is hard to know how to set about arguing against the person mentioned at the end of the last paragraph, it is hard to know how to set about arguing against this person. Suppose he says that one ought always to do what God wills. We may reply that there is no God and that there cannot therefore be any obligation to do what he wills. Or we may say that there is no way of knowing what God wills. But unless we can substantiate these claims it seems that there is little more to be said. We may argue with our opponent; we may put to him the possibility of God willing various actions, and we may provide reasons for holding that these actions are immoral. But if the opponent's fundamental premise is that one is morally bound to do what God wills, I do not see that we are going to get very far. In saying this I do not just mean that we are unlikely to change our opponent's mind. I mean that we shall not be able to convict him of error. For in trying to combat his views we shall ultimately have to adopt moral positions that are themselves as basic and unsupported as his. Someone who says that God's will is the fundamental criterion for determining whether an action is moral is asserting a fundamental premise in his thinking. And in contesting his thinking we can only assert our own fundamental premises. And looked at from this point of view our position need be no more demonstrably correct than his.

I would argue, then, that (1) may or may not be acceptable depending on our fundamental moral options and depending on whether it is possible to say that there is a God whose will can be known. But what about (2)?

Anyone familiar with twentieth-century moral philosophy will at once realize that there is a standard defence of (2) likely to be advanced by some philosophers. According to some writers there is a difference between statements of fact (such as 'God wills X') and statements of value (such as 'I ought to do X'). These writers would add that statements of value cannot be derived from statements of fact. They would therefore argue that just because God wills something nothing whatever follows about what ought to be done.

But even if these writers are correct it can still be held that God's will can determine what is morally obligatory. The reason for saying so takes us back to what I have just said about (1). For while it is obviously invalid to argue from

God wills that P should do X

to

P should do X,

someone who says that God's will can determine what is morally obligatory may not just be arguing in this way. He may argue:

(*a*) God wills that P should do X.
(*b*) One is morally obliged to do what God wills.
(*c*) Therefore P should do X.

As far as I can see this is a perfectly valid argument. If it were used with reference to a particular person and action one might reject it by denying that there is a God whose will can be known. And if one could show that one was right then the case against (2) would be made. But if one could not do so one would have to say that (*b*) was false. Yet that, as I have already suggested, is not very easy to do. I therefore suggest that (2) is a maintainable position, and that, for this reason, and supposing that there is a God whose will can be known, (2) is a possible position for someone to adopt.

It seems, then, that there is something to be said for the view that morality is included in religion; but not, perhaps, for all versions of this view. Earlier on I noted the position of R. B. Braithwaite, according to whom morality is included in religion in a fairly distinctive way. But is Braithwaite's account plausible?

In defence of Braithwaite it might be said that there is surely a close connection between what we normally call 'moral beliefs' and beliefs which appear incontrovertibly religious. The New Testament, for example, insists on the value of certain kinds of behaviour which many non-religious people would normally regard as morally binding. Braithwaite talks of religious belief in terms of commitment to action, and here, too, it might be urged that he has a point. It is surely true that religious people commit themselves to ways of behaving.

But Braithwaite appears to regard religious belief as essentially a matter of commitment to behaviour, and herein lies a major difficulty with his thesis. As we have seen, he associates with religious belief the entertainment of certain 'stories', which he calls 'straightforwardly empirical propositions' (i.e. propositions whose truth could in principle be checked by sense experience). And these stories include such statements as 'God exists', 'Man is justified by the Atonement wrought through Christ', 'Christians are doing the will of God', and 'There are three persons in the Trinity.'[16]   But according to Braithwaite religious believers do not have to believe these stories. 'What I am calling a *story*', he explains, 'Matthew Arnold called a *parable* and a *fairy-tale*. Other terms which might be used are *allegory, fable, tale, myth*. . . . A man is not, I think, a professing Christian unless he both proposes to live according to Christian moral principles and associates his intention with thinking of Christian stories; but he need not believe that the empirical propositions presented by the stories correspond to empirical fact.'[17] As well as committing themselves to policies of action, however, many religious believers say that they believe in certain facts. The Christian, for example, not only believes that he should act in accordance with Christian moral principles; he also believes that there is a God.

One certainly needs to approach the topic of religious facts with caution. When we think of facts we normally think of arrangements of objects in the physical universe, and it is fairly clear that one cannot talk as if religious believers only believed in facts of this kind. What about 'There is a God' or 'Henry is in a state of grace'? Presumably Henry's state of grace is not entirely open to public investigation. Perhaps it might be said to show itself in Henry's behaviour; but 'Henry is in a state of grace' still seems on a different level from 'Henry is in a state of tension.' And while 'There is a God' may sound remarkably like 'There is a President', it is also very different. Presidents are locatable in space, but God is not usually thought of in this way. Christians might say that God is everywhere; but they would normally reject the suggestion that he is in my pocket as is my money.

So the notion of religious facts is a puzzling one. But it also seems clear that most religious believers do regard religious statements as factual in some sense. And it can at least minimally be said that statements like 'There is a God' are most often intended to do more than announce allegiance to a policy of action. Otherwise it would be hard to account for disagreement over religious matters. When, for example, people say that they believe in God they would normally regard themselves as contradicting those who say that there is no God. Spelling out the kind of contradiction involved in such a dispute may be a difficult undertaking, but it is surely relevant. In terms of Braithwaite's position, however, the task of exposition could never even begin to arise. Even if we allow for its reference to 'stories', Braithwaite's position seems to ignore the fact that religious statements are often more than statements about people's behaviour. In *Words and Images*,[18] E. L. Mascall tells a story about a Frenchman who went to a lecture and asked whether what he had just been offered in it was a religion in which one did not need to believe in God. The lecturer replied that it was. 'Religion sans Dieu', retorted the questioner. 'Mon Dieu, quelle religion!' Mascall feels that Braithwaite's exposition might justifiably provoke a similar reaction; and, though there are evidently religions which do not subscribe to anything that could be called belief in God, he surely has a point.

Is morality opposed to religion?

I have so far argued both for and against various versions of the view that morality is included in religion. Now it remains to consider the assertion that morality is opposed to religion. In noting forms that this assertion has taken I began earlier on by indicating the view of James Rachels, according to whom (*a*) one can disprove God's existence on moral grounds, and (*b*) someone who believes in God cannot be an autonomous moral agent. So let us first turn to Rachels's position.

Perhaps the first thing to be said about it is that, considered as a disproof of God's existence, it is very weak indeed. For Rachels seems to suppose that if there is a being worthy of worship then there could not be autonomous moral agents. But there is an obvious reply to this supposition. For it is surely possible that there be a being worthy of worship who does nothing to interfere with people who wish to remain autonomous moral agents. And it is also possible that a being worthy of worship will require that people always act as autonomous moral agents. This point is well brought out in a case against Rachels offered by Philip L. Quinn in his book *Divine Commands and Moral Requirements*. As he observes:

An autonomous moral agent can admit the existence of God if he is prepared to deny that any putative divine command which is inconsistent with his hard-core reflective moral judgements really is a divine command. He can resolve the supposed role-conflict by allowing that genuine divine commands ought to be obeyed unconditionally but also maintaining that no directive which he does not accept on moral grounds is a genuine divine command. For the following propositions are logically compatible:

(20) God exists.

(21) God sometimes commands agents to do certain things.

(22) God never commands anything an autonomous and well-informed human moral agent would, on reflection, disapprove.[19]

Yet might it not be argued that if a being is worthy of worship then the worshipper is bound to do what the being wills? And does not this mean that being a worshipper is incompatible with being an autonomous moral agent? Evidently Rachels supposes that the answer to these questions is affirmative. But it is not such at all. For a worshipper can consistently say that what he worships is a being who always wills him to behave as an autonomous moral agent. And if a worshipper were to say this then Rachels's case would clearly collapse. For it rests on the premise that a person can only regard as worthy of worship a being whose will does not entail that the person ceases to be an autonomous moral agent.

But this does not mean that morality and religion are not always opposed. Yet does the thesis that they are opposed really make sense? There is a case for denying that it does.

One reason for saying so is that the word 'morality' evidently has different associations for different people. What one person regards as morality another may dismiss as immorality or as just plain triviality. And it often seems impossible to say that either party in such disputes is in some objective sense right. General statements about what morality is should be regarded with suspicion, for the boundaries dividing the moral and the non-moral may be very fuzzy indeed. And for this reason one ought to be suspicious about the general and very sweeping statement that religion and morality are necessarily opposed to each other.

A second reason for rejecting this statement brings us to a related point regarding the term 'religion'. If I say that religion and morality are opposed to each other, I assume that there is a fairly easily identifiable thing called 'religion'. But this assumption is very questionable indeed. In Henry Fielding's novel *Tom Jones* Mr Thwackum declares: 'When I mention religion I mean the Christian religion; and not only the Christian religion but the Protestant religion; and not only the Protestant religion, but the Church of England.' Yet few philosophers or theologians would be happy to accept this definition since it seems to exclude so much. Many writers, in fact, would go so far as to say that 'religion' just cannot be defined. 'It is', says Ninian Smart, 'partly a matter of convention as to what is counted under the head of religion and what is not.'[20] Here Smart is in agreement with what William P. Alston writes on 'Religion' in *The Encyclopedia of Philosophy*.[21] Alston notes various attempts to define 'religion' and concludes that none of them states necessary and sufficient conditions for something to be a religion. He concludes that the most that can be done is to note various characteristics of religion.

When enough of these characteristics are present to a sufficient degree, we have a religion. It seems that, given the actual use of the term 'religion', this is as precise as we can be. If we tried to say something like 'for a religion to exist, there must be the first two plus any three others', or 'for a religion to exist, any four of these characteristics must be present', we would be introducing a degree of precision not to be found in the concept of religion actually in use . . . the best way to explain the concept of religion is to elaborate in detail the relevant features of an ideally clear case of religion and then indicate the respects in which less clear cases can differ from this, without hoping to find any sharp line dividing religion from non-religion.

The implication of such reflections is that it is misleading to say that religion and morality are necessarily opposed to each other. And this means that we can call into question statements like that of Russell noted earlier. A great deal that he considered harmful may well have been done by people in the name of religion. But many religious people would accept this fact while objecting to the very things to which Russell objected. They would, in fact, argue that many of the key values for which Russell stood are an essential part of religious aspiration. Thus, and returning to the precise points made by Russell in his remark quoted earlier, there are, for example, Christians who argue strongly in favour of pluralistic and open education, for pacifism and for scientific co-operation. And all this on theological grounds.

But it ought to be added that there are evidently religious believers whose religious beliefs entail for them moral judgements sharply at odds with those adopted by many moral thinkers. And sometimes it may be quite impossible to resolve the resulting conflict. Take, for instance, the conflict between many secular moralists and those theologians who hold certain views about topics like divorce because they think that they have access to divinely inspired words of Christ. These secular moralists and theologians often seem to share a great deal of common ground regarding criteria for making various moral judgements; but they can evidently reach deadlock in the long run because one group thinks that sound moral teaching has been revealed by God while the other does not. And until they can come to agree on matters like that of revelation no solution to their final disagreement seems possible.

This kind of thing may, of course, lead one to ask whether religion does not, after all, demand some kind of view opposed to anything that can be regarded as a moral one. But this is not a question to answer in general terms and indeed I doubt whether it is very clear to begin with. As should be evident from the diversity of views referred to in this chapter, anyone concerned with the relationship between morality and religion will need to proceed slowly and with reference to various understandings of both morality and religion.

11 Miracle

One word that often creeps into the active vocabulary of religious people is 'miracle'. Many would say that miracles occur or that they have occurred. It is also sometimes suggested that they provide evidence for various things, notably the existence of God or the truth of some particular religion or the teaching of particular religious leaders. The topic of miracle has occasioned considerable philosophical debate and it therefore seems appropriate at this point to say something about it.

What is a miracle?

Perhaps the obvious question to turn to at the outset is that of the nature of miracles. What are we discussing when we talk about miracles? Actually, the answer is not all that obvious, for those who refer to miracles have offered various understandings of what it is that they are talking about.

One widespread view of miracles sees them as breaks in the natural order of events in the material world. Sometimes these breaks are referred to as violations of natural laws and it is often said that these breaks or violations are brought about by God or by some extremely powerful being whose action can interfere with the normal course of nature's operation. A classic definition of 'miracle' given in these terms comes from David Hume who wrote on miracles in Chapter X of his *Enquiry concerning Human Understanding*. 'A miracle', says Hume, 'may be accurately defined, *a transgression of a law of nature by a particular volition of the Deity or by the interposition of some invisible agent.*'[1] A related account of 'miracle' is offered by Aquinas. 'Those things must properly be called miraculous', he writes in the *Summa Contra Gentiles*, 'which are done by divine power apart from the order generally followed in things.'[2] In this connection Aquinas distinguishes between various kinds of miracle. The first embraces 'those events in which something is done by God which nature could never do'.[3] Among the examples cited by Aquinas is a reversal in the course of the sun. Secondly, he refers to 'events in which God does something which nature can do, but not in this order'. As an example of what he has in mind here Aquinas cites the case of someone walking after being struck by paralysis. Finally, he singles out as miraculous that which 'occurs when God does what is usually done by the working of nature, but without the operation of the principles of nature'. In this connection Aquinas refers to a person being cured by divine power of a fever which could be cured naturally.[4]

Here, then, is a fairly strong understanding of miracles, as events which cannot be explained in terms intelligible to the natural scientist or observer of the regular processes of nature. But other less strong meanings have been given to 'miracle'. In English translations of the Bible, for example, 'miracle' is sometimes used to refer only to an event which the author regards as somehow significant or as somehow pointing beyond itself. 'The Bible', as R. H. Fuller points out, 'knows nothing of nature as a closed system of law. Indeed the very word "nature" is unbiblical.... The biblical view of miracles runs counter to the accepted view of miracle as an occurrence contrary to the laws of nature or to what is known of nature.'[5] It is also possible to find a weaker understanding of 'miracle' given in such a way that 'miracle' means only 'extraordinary coincidence of a beneficial nature'. One can find this understanding at work in a well-known article by R. F. Holland. He begins by telling the following story:

A child riding his toy motor-car strays on to an unguarded railway crossing near his house and a wheel of his car gets stuck down the side of one of the rails. An express train is due to pass with the signals in its favour and a curve in the track makes it impossible for the driver to stop his train in time to avoid any obstruction he might encounter on the crossing. The mother coming out of the house to look for her child sees him on the crossing and hears the train approaching. She runs forward shouting and waving. The little boy remains seated in his car looking downward engrossed in the task of pedalling it free. The brakes of the train are applied and it comes to rest a few feet from the child. The mother thanks God for the miracle; which she never ceases to think of as such although, as she in due course learns, there was nothing supernatural about the manner in which the brakes of the train came to be applied. The driver had fainted, for a reason that had nothing to do with the presence of the child on the line, and the brakes were applied automatically as his hand ceased to exert pressure on the control lever. He fainted on this particular afternoon because his blood pressure had risen after an exceptionally heavy lunch during which he had quarrelled with a colleague, and the change in blood pressure caused a clot of blood to be dislodged and circulate. He fainted at the time when he did on the afternoon in question because this was the time at which the coagulation in his blood stream reached the brain.[6]

Commenting on this story, Holland notes that it can be regarded as miraculous from the religious point of view. In certain circumstances, he says, 'a coincidence can be taken religiously as a sign and called a miracle.' But, Holland adds, 'it cannot without confusion be taken as a sign of divine interference with the natural order.'[7]

So miracles have been understood in different ways. But what are we to make of them in general? To phrase the question in a more obviously philosophical way: on any of the above senses of 'miracle' is it reasonable to believe in miracles? Let us begin to consider this question by turning first to the strong sense of 'miracle', which I shall call 'S-miracle'. Here two questions need to be asked. First, are S-miracles possible? Secondly, is there any reason to believe that any have occurred?

The possibility of S-miracles

It has been argued that S-miracles are quite straightforwardly impossible. The idea here is not that they are hard to imagine happening but rather that the whole notion of an S-miracle is logically self-contradictory. Traces of this view can be found in Chapter X of Hume's *Enquiry concerning Human Understanding*. For most of this chapter Hume's main interest lies in arguing, possibly in reply to a work called *Tryal of the Witnesses of the Resurrection*,[8] that reports of S-miracles are not to be trusted. But occasionally he seems to be suggesting something more. At one point, for instance, he refers to reports of miracles performed at the tomb of the Abbé Paris. 'And what have we to oppose to such a cloud of witnesses, but the absolute impossibility or miraculous nature of the events, which they relate? And this surely, in the eyes of all reasonable people, will alone be regarded as a sufficient refutation.'[9]

But Hume's position here is surely very dubious. For while we may have good reason to believe that any reported S-miracle has not occurred, it is surely logically possible that one should occur. Suppose we put on our creative writing caps and dream up a story about Gertrude. She is suffering from incurable cancer. All the best doctors have pronounced her doomed to die. The cancer has already virtually eaten her up. But one morning she wakes up fit and well. And all the doctors agree that she is fit and well, that something has happened which as far as they are concerned cannot happen. Now for various reasons we may be sceptical if someone told us that Gertrude actually did undergo this wonder-cure. But there is no logical incoherence in the notion of her having done so. 'Gertrude was in the last stages of cancer and then suddenly recovered' may be incredible, but it is surely very different from 'The square circle kicked the Bishop and married the undertaker's daughter.' Hume's remark about the absolute impossibility of S-miracles seems to overlook this point.

It also seems to overlook the fact that it is not inconceivable to imagine circumstances which would, if they occurred, make it reasonable to talk in terms of a violation of a law of nature.

Some philosophers, not perhaps uninfluenced by Hume himself, would be thoroughly opposed to this suggestion. It seems to presuppose that it is reasonable to talk about laws of nature, but many writers have contested this suggestion. They would argue, for example, that just because we have regularly observed a certain series of events we have no good reason for believing that these events must go together. We expect to find them together, but there is no guarantee that they will actually be together and therefore no guarantee that we are justified in talking in terms of laws of nature.

But, if we are talking about what it is and is not reasonable to believe, such a line of argument is open to objection. Certainly, what we expect to be the case may fail to be the case; it is not, perhaps, absurd to suggest that the water put over the flame may one day turn to ice instead of heating up, and this in spite of what we have so far observed. But we should hardly be reasonable in acting on such a principle. We should normally be inclined to say, in fact, that it is the mark of a rational man to act otherwise. Such action certainly seems to square with reasoning that is of fundamental importance in scientific inquiry. Fundamental to such inquiry is the principle that the course of nature continues uniformly the same and that if events of type A regularly follow events of type B in one set of circumstances, then other events of type A can be held to follow other events of type B in more or less identical circumstances unless there is some relevant difference that can itself be understood in terms of some covering law. We can express this point by saying that there is no obvious reason why we should rationally refuse to talk about laws of nature. To say that there are laws of nature is to say that reality is intelligible in the sense that the behaviour of physical things can be predicted. Things behave in regular ways and it is possible to frame scientific explanations and expectations. It may be held that the behaviour of many things is extremely irregular. One might appeal here to quantum physics and its talk about the random motions of fundamental particles. But at the macroscopic level it still seems that we can reasonably talk about laws; it still seems that we can talk the language of statistics and probability. We can say that when human beings suffer massive heart attacks they can reasonably be expected to die. We can say that when you boil an egg for half an hour you can reasonably expect to get a hard-boiled egg.

But does it follow that we can never reasonably say that there has occurred a violation of a natural law? Initially we might have very good reason for doubting that a particular natural law has been violated; and confronted with what appears to be good testimony that it has in fact been violated we might therefore attempt to account for the phenomena appealed to in some way that does not contradict the principle that laws of nature are not violated. Thus, if someone says that an incredible cure has occurred, we might seek to explain what has been observed by bringing it under some other well-established law. And in default of any such known law we might just refuse to accept that there has been a violation of a law of nature, and we might say that there is some law in operation but that we are so far ignorant of it. But it is not inconceivable that such a way of proceeding could land us in more difficulties than we would solve. Suppose that some event occurs and is monitored by strict scientific methods. Let us suppose that some amazing planetary motion is observed and that the whole process is noted by the most reputable scientists in the world. If we now say that this event can be explained in terms of some law of nature, we will evidently have to show that it exemplifies some previously noted phenomena and is understandable. But it may be that nobody observing it would say that it does exemplify some previously noted phenomena – at least, not in the sense that it exemplifies any phenomena reported and assimilated by scientists. If we want to deny that any natural law has been violated in this case, we will therefore have to revise our theories about the behaviour of the planets. The trouble now is that it might be enormously expensive (intellectually, not financially) to do so. We might have to agree, for example, that in accordance with perfectly natural laws it is more than conceivable that the planets should behave in the way observed on the occasion now in question. And such a position might play havoc with a vast amount of scientific theory. In such circumstances it might, in fact, be more economical and more reasonable to accept that a law of nature has been violated. But if this is correct, it follows that a law of nature can reasonably be said to be violated and that Hume is wrong to say that S-miracles are absolutely impossible.

Nor does it seem that this conclusion of Hume's is entirely consistent with some other things that he says. As we saw in Chapter 5, he denies any necessary connection between cause and effect. So how can he be so sure that certain reported events, like those said to have occurred at the tomb of the Abbé Paris, could never happen? Antony Flew suggests that when Hume declares that certain miracles are 'impossible' he means that they are physically impossible, not logically impossible. Flew adds that 'the criterion of physical as opposed to logical impossibility simply is logical incompatibility with a law of nature in the broadest sense.[10] But in that case Hume is saying either that certain events do not happen or that what is said to happen conflicts with what we take to be laws of nature. But the first suggestion is not equivalent to the assertion that certain events could not happen and is in any case simply over-dogmatic and hardly a proof of anything relevant to a philosophical discussion of miracles. And the second suggestion seems open to the reply that what we take to be a law of nature may just not be so. This point is well brought out by J. C. A. Gaskin:

Consider an example. Hume could have said (with complete justification) that it was physically impossible, according to the best nomologicals [propositions stating supposed laws of nature] at his disposal, for a man in England to be able to talk to and see a man who is at the same time in America. Now if he had taken this to mean 'it could not happen that . . .' then we would simply retort it *has* happened. In short, if we are to employ the notion of physical impossibility, the most this can mean is that: within 'our' experience of the world the event has not happened, nor are we able to conceive how it could happen, nor could it possibly happen *if* the laws of nature have in fact the form and content which we attribute to them. What force then has such impossibility got as used by a 'just reasoner' against a report of a miracle? No more force than Hume's original argument that the event is against all our past and what we presume to be our invariable experience. That is, there is a strong and rational presumption against the event but not a demonstration of its 'absolute impossibility' in any sense of that phrase in which it can be taken to imply '*could not happen*'.[11]

And, as Gaskin goes on to note, Hume is not totally unaware of this. For at one point in his discussion of miracles Hume observes: 'I beg the limitations here made may be remarked, when I say, that a miracle can never be proved, so as to be the foundation of a system of religion. For I own, that otherwise, there may possibly be miracles, or violations of the usual course of nature, of such a kind as to admit of proof from human testimony; though, perhaps, it will be impossible to find any such in all the records of history.'[12]

But there is another line of argument open to a writer like Hume, one which we have not yet touched on. Hume's doubtful remark about the absolute impossibility of miracles is based on a difficulty in believing that (at least some) laws of nature can be violated. But an S-miracle might be defined as something brought about by God or by some very powerful being other than God. Might it not therefore be said that there is something absolutely impossible about an S-miracle in this sense?

As the reader must well realize by now, some philosophers would say that it might. Anybody impressed by the attacks on belief in God discussed in Chapters 1 to 3 would argue that it is impossible to maintain the existence of God, so he would presumably have to say that it is impossible that there should be an S-miracle, if such a thing has to be brought about by God. And, given a view of God according to which God has the attributes discussed in Chapters 8 and 9, and given a person who thinks that God cannot exist with these attributes, we would expect to find a rejection of S-miracles, if these, by definition, are brought about by God.

At this point the reader must consider his reaction to what I have been arguing in this book about the existence and attributes of God. And if he concludes that my arguments are unacceptable, he may wish to defend the view that S-miracles are strictly speaking impossible if thought of as brought about by God.

If, however, what I have earlier argued stands, or if there is a reason for believing in the possibility or reality of God of which I have said nothing, then there does not seem to be any obvious impossibility in the occurrence of an S-miracle. A very powerful cause of the existence of things could surely bring it about that natural laws which regularly hold should, on some occasion, fail to do so only to be replaced by an event that is reasonably characterized as a violation of them – on condition, of course, that this event is itself a possible state of affairs. In this connection it is worth noting some observations of Aquinas. He asks whether God can 'do anything outside the order inherent in creation' (*aliquid praeter ordinem rebus inditum*), and he says that God can since he is responsible for creation in the first place and since no natural power makes him act as he does. 'If ', says Aquinas, 'we take the order in things as it depends on the secondary causes,[13] then God can act apart from it; he is not subject to that order but rather it is subject to him, as issuing from him not out of a necessity of nature, but by decision of his will. . . . Hence when he so wills, he can act apart from the given order, producing, for example, the effects of secondary causes without them or some effects that surpass the powers of these causes.'[14]

As for the possibility of the notion of an S-miracle being brought about by some very powerful agent, much here depends on whether it is possible for there to be any agent who is not part of the physical universe. But, as I argued with reference to the design argument, the notion of intelligent extra-mundane agency is not impossible. And, as Swinburne argues in *The Concept of Miracle*, there could well be circumstances that made it reasonable to say that some violation of a natural law is brought about by something like a human agent or agents. Let E be a violation of a natural law. Then:

suppose that E occurs in ways and circumstances otherwise strongly analogous to those in which occur events brought about intentionally by human agents, and that other violations occur in such circumstances. We would then be justified in claiming that E and other such violations are, like effects of human actions, brought about by agents, but agents unlike men in not being material objects. This inference would be justified because, if an analogy between effects is strong enough, we are always justified in postulating slight difference in causes to account for slight difference in effects.[15]

The reasonableness of believing in S-miracles

I suggest, then, that S-miracles are possible. But is it reasonable to believe that any have occurred? Hume provides what is probably the most famous discussion of this question, again in Chapter X of the *Enquiry concerning Human Understanding*. So let us look at what he says.

To begin with he states a fundamental principle. When a wise man is conducting an inquiry, says Hume, he 'proportions his belief to the evidence'.[16] When he talks of 'evidence' here Hume is thinking about the results of empirical inquiry. Thus he argues that:

A miracle is a violation of the laws of nature; and as a firm and unalterable experience has established these laws, the proof against a miracle, from the very nature of the fact, is as entire as any argument from experience can possibly be imagined. Why is it more than probable, that all men must die; that lead cannot, of itself, remain suspended in the air; that fire consumes wood, and is extinguished by water; unless it be, that these events are found agreeable to the laws of nature, and there is required a violation of these laws, or in other words, a miracle to prevent them?[17]

Hume allows that many witnesses may testify that a miraculous event has occurred. But, he adds, 'no testimony is sufficient to establish a miracle unless the testimony be of such kind, that its falsehood would be more miraculous, than the fact, which it endeavours to establish; and even in that case there is a mutual destruction of arguments, and the superior only gives us assurance to that degree of force, which remains, after deducting the inferior.'[18]

In sum, therefore, Hume is arguing as follows. A miracle is a violation of a law of nature. We have very good evidence, based on experience, that laws of nature hold. This evidence must oblige us to disregard reports about the occurrence of miracles.

In addition to this argument, however, Hume also has some other points to make. He is concerned to ask whether we can accept that a miracle has occurred, and he is chiefly interested in the question of relying on testimony that some miracles have occurred. As he develops his case, therefore, it is to the reliability of testimony in favour of miracles that Hume turns his attention. Here he makes four points, designed, as he puts it, to show that 'there never was a miraculous event established.'[19]

The first is that no reported miracle comes with the testimony of enough people who can be regarded as sufficiently intelligent, learned, reputable, and so on to justify us in believing reports of miracles.

There is not to be found, in all history, any miracle attested by a sufficient number of men, of such unquestioned good-sense, education, and learning, as to secure us against all delusion in themselves; of such undoubted integrity, as to place them beyond all suspicion of any design to deceive others; of such credit and reputation in the eyes of mankind, as to have a great deal to lose in case of their being detected in any falsehood; and at the same time, attesting facts performed in such a public manner and in so celebrated a part of the world, as to render the detection unavoidable.[20]

The second point is that people are naturally prone to look for marvels and wonders and that this must be taken as giving us grounds for being sceptical of reported miracles. 'We may', says Hume,

observe in human nature a principle which, if strictly examined, will be found to diminish extremely the assurance, which we might, from human testimony, have, in any kind of prodigy. . . . The passion of *surprise* and *wonder*, arising from miracles, being an agreeable emotion, gives a sensible tendency towards the belief of those events, from which it is derived. And this goes so far, that even those who cannot enjoy this pleasure immediately, nor can believe those miraculous events, of which they are informed, yet love to partake of the satisfaction at second-hand or by rebound, and place a pride and delight in exciting the admiration of others.[21]

In this connection Hume adds that religious people are particularly untrustworthy. 'A religionist', he says, 'may be an enthusiast, and imagine he sees what has no reality: he may know his narrative to be false, and yet persevere in it, with the best intentions in the world, for the sake of promoting so holy a cause.'[22] Religious people, Hume says, are subject to vanity, self-interest, and impudence.[23] He also points out that 'The many instances of forged miracles, and prophecies, and supernatural events which, in all ages, have either been detected by contrary evidence, or which detect themselves by their absurdity, prove sufficiently the strong propensity of mankind to the extraordinary and the marvellous, and ought reasonably to beget a suspicion against all relations of this kind.'[24]

Thirdly, Hume claims that 'It forms a strong presumption against all supernatural and miraculous relations that they are observed chiefly to abound among ignorant and barbarous nations.'[25]

Hume's final point is rather more complicated. Basically he is arguing in this way. If Fred, Bill, and John testify that there is a kangaroo in the bathroom, and if Mabel, Mary, and Catherine testify that there is no kangaroo in the bathroom, then the testimonies cancel each other out and neither should be accepted. In the case of miracles, different religions report different miracles. These reports must be viewed as contradicting each other. Therefore, if any religious person testifies to the occurrence of a miracle within his religious tradition, the testimony can safely be ignored since there are plenty of other reports of the occurrence of miracles within different religious traditions and the two sets of reports cancel each other out. In Hume's own words:

To make this the better understood, let us consider that, in matters of religion, whatever is different is contrary, and that it is impossible the religions of ancient Rome, of Turkey, of Siam, and of China should, all of them, be established on any solid foundation. Every miracle, therefore, pretended to have been wrought in any of these religions (and all of them abound in miracles), as its direct scope is to establish the particular system to which it is attributed; so has it the same force, though more indirectly, to overthrow every other system. In destroying a rival system, it likewise destroys the credit of those miracles, on which that system was established.[26]

Here, then, are Hume's arguments against its being reasonable to hold that an S-miracle has occurred. But are they good arguments?

People sometimes maintain that Hume's arguments about miracles are suspect since they do not cope with the possibility that one might person-ally witness a miracle. This suggestion is both sensible and misguided. It is sensible in view of what I have already argued about the possibility of S-miracles. If the argument of the preceding section is correct, then there could be an S-miracle and we could reasonably believe that there had been such a thing. And, of course, this would be an even more reasonable view if we already had good evidence to believe in a God likely to bring about S-miracles. But the suggestion is misguided if taken as a successful rebut-tal of Hume's arguments in Chapter X of the *Enquiry concerning Human Understanding*. For Hume's target there is not really X's belief that what he has experienced makes it reasonable for him to believe that an S-miracle has occurred. One has, of course, to reckon with Hume's strong state-ments about what is absolutely impossible, but, allowing for the basic thrust of his discussion, we can agree with Gaskin's comment that 'Hume's argument tells me that if *I* have seen a miracle I should not expect any reasonable or wise man to believe my report. . . . Hume is simply warning that incredulity is what I should expect. His argument refers explicitly and totally to the credibility of reports of miracles not to the possibility of actually experiencing one take place.'[27]

So the question before us is really whether Hume has given sufficient reason for disregarding the testimony of others offered in support of S-miracles. And to begin with it has surely to be allowed that many of Hume's points give one good reason for approaching any report of an S-miracle with a measure of caution. As he says, for instance, in deciding what probably happened it is reasonable in general to be guided by our knowledge of what regularly happens. And it is certainly true that there are hosts of authenticated fraudulent reports of S-miracles. Furthermore, many of the best-known reports of S-miracles do not come with the testi-mony of large numbers of people and they emerge from groups or societies in parts of the world where one might expect to find people giving easy credence to reports of marvels and wonders. Anybody familiar with con-temporary biblical scholarship will know that this is so, for example, in the case of reported wonders in the Bible.

But Hume's discussion of miracles and testimony still contains problematic elements. For example, at crucial stages in his argument he seems to ignore some obvious questions. He says that history does not provide testimony to the miraculous from 'a sufficient number of men, of such unquestioned good sense, education, and learning as to secure us against all delusion in themselves'. But how many men constitute a sufficient number? And what counts as good sense, education, and learning? Later on in his text Hume accuses people of being swayed by their love of the wonderful. No doubt many people are swayed in this way, but is it absolutely evident that everybody who has reported the occurrence of an S-miracle has been thus swayed? And is there really good evidence that religious people cannot distinguish truth from error in the case of the marvellous, that they are always governed by their concern to back the religious cause?

In the nature of the case it seems exceedingly difficult to answer such questions. So much depends on taking particular cases and examining them in considerable detail. I think it can be said, however, that Hume is rather premature in supposing that the observations which he makes are sufficient to justify us in concluding that we can always disregard testimony to the effect that a miracle, in Hume's sense, has occurred. For one thing, he seems to have forgotten the possibility of corroborating what someone claims to have occurred. But past events sometimes leave physical traces which survive into the present. It may thus be urged against Hume that it is conceivable that some reported S-miracle can be reasonably believed to have occurred because of what can be gleaned from some physical data in the present. Even in default of such data, and unless one is determined to insist that nobody can be taken as a reliable witness of what actually occurs, it can be said that there is no reason why the existence of laws of nature should force us to conclude that somebody who reports the violation of a natural law must be misreporting. One may grant that particular instances need to be examined very carefully indeed, and in reading Hume's discussion of miracles one can see exactly why. But how can one rule out in advance the possibility of rationally concluding that somebody (or several people) who reported a violation of a natural law was providing an accurate description of what occurred and providing in doing so a description of something that could most reasonably be interpreted as a violation of a natural law?

An objector might reply that there still remains the point about reports of miracles made from different religions. But here again Hume seems to be moving too fast. In his own day it was widely assumed that the reported miracles in the New Testament established the truth of Christianity and the absolute falsehood of all other religions. But why should we assume that if we have reports of miracles from, for example, a Christian and a Hindu, both reports cannot be accepted as reports of miracles which actually occurred? Hume seems to assume some such principle as: 'If a Christian miracle occurs, that is evidence against the truth of Hinduism. And if a Hindu miracle occurs, that is evidence against the truth of Christianity.' But this principle does not seem necessarily true. As Swinburne argues, 'evidence for a miracle "wrought in one religion" is only evidence against the occurrence of a miracle "wrought in another religion" if the two miracles, if they occurred, would be evidence for propositions of the two religious systems incompatible with each other.'[28]

It seems, then, that, considered as an argument against the reasonableness of ever believing any report to the effect that an S-miracle has occurred, Hume's discussion is indecisive. And there, I think, we may profitably leave the question of believing in reports of S-miracles, for, as I am myself arguing, any positive conclusions about the reasonableness of believing that S-miracles have occurred would have to result from a study of circumstantial detail.

Miracles as signs or coincidence

I have now considered miracle as understood in one way. And I have considered it at length because this understanding is the one that has given rise to most philosophical discussion. But it still remains to be asked whether it is reasonable to believe in miracles when these are considered as signs or coincidences.

If one looks at biblical uses of the word 'sign' it soon becomes apparent that, even though biblical writers do not, as Fuller says, have a concept of 'nature', the word is applied to events that look like remarkably good candidates for the title 'violation of a law of nature'. Such, for example, is the case with St. John's application of 'sign' as a description of Jesus turning water into wine. If, however, it is solidly maintained that a miracle is only a sign in that it is an event into which it is possible to read significance, or an event that somehow points beyond itself, then it is very hard indeed to show that belief in miracles is either reasonable or unreasonable. For, surely, 'significance' can mean almost anything at all, as can 'points beyond itself'. It might be said that there are surely events that are significant from a religious point of view. And this would be very hard to deny, for religious people seem capable of reading significance into almost anything. It might also be said that some events 'point beyond themselves' in religiously significant ways. And this too would be hard to deny given that 'point beyond' is an extremely vague expression the legitimate uses of which seem very hard to circumscribe.

But when 'miracle' means 'coincidence' there are surely fewer problems. For we all know that coincidences occur and most of us would be prepared to believe in a story like that told by Holland should it appear in a reputable daily newspaper. The only questions one feels bound to raise are: (1) is there any point in giving the name 'miracle' to coincidences like that imagined by Holland; (2) is there any justification for thanking God for such coincidences?

It seems to me that Holland himself provides a perfectly acceptable answer to the first question. He observes that certain coincidences (which he calls 'contingencies') 'can be and are in fact regarded religiously in the manner I have indicated'. In other words, religious people do sometimes refer to certain extraordinary coincidences as miracles. And as far as I can see there is no decisive reason why they should not. In the history of philosophy and theology 'miracle' has largely meant 'highly unusual event', though it has also usually meant more. Witness the accounts of Aquinas and Hume. But an extraordinary coincidence *is* a highly unusual event, and it seems to involve no massive perpetration of a linguistic barbarism for someone to apply the term 'miracle' to it. Though perhaps a great deal depends on what kind of coincidence is involved.

But whether there is any justification for thanking God for such highly extraordinary coincidences as that imagined by Holland is a more difficult matter to comment on. It depends, for one thing, on whether one thinks it reasonable to believe in God. But, in concluding this all too brief discussion of miracles, one point at least can be made. To thank God for a highly extraordinary event must surely involve supposing that God is in some sense causally involved in it. If, then, it is reasonable to regard God as the cause of all existing things, then it is reasonable to regard him as causally involved in extraordinary coincidences. For these are only made up of existing things. In other words, it is not too hard to see how one might reasonably move from 'This is an extraordinary event' to 'This is something in which God is causally involved.'

12 Life after death

We have now looked at various topics and questions commonly discussed by philosophers of religion. And there are many more that will have to be considered by anyone who proposes to deal seriously with the philosophy of religion. But not all of these can be considered in this book. We ought, however, to pay some attention to the problem of life after death, for that is of fundamental importance for many religious people and has provoked a lot of philosophical attention. Belief in life after death has taken many forms, some of which are unique to particular religious systems though others can be found in more than one religion. In this chapter it is impossible to touch on all of them, but two in particular have been much adhered to and much discussed by philosophers. Perhaps, then, we can turn to these.

Two views of life after death

The first of our views about life after death certainly has a venerable philosophical history. It can be found, for example, in Plato's *Phaedo*. Here we are presented with the figure of Socrates who is about to drink poison because he has been condemned to death. His friends are grief-stricken, but Socrates assures them that he is perfectly capable of surviving death. One of Socrates' friends, a man called Crito, asks 'And in what way shall we bury you?'

In any way you like; but you must get hold of me, and take care that I do not run away from you. Then he turned to us, and added with a smile: – I cannot make Crito believe that I am the same Socrates who has been talking and conducting the argument; he fancies that I am the other Socrates whom he will soon see, a dead body – and he asks, How shall he bury me? And though I have spoken many words in the endeavour to show that when I have drunk the poison I shall leave you and go to the joys of the blessed, – these words of mine, with which I was comforting you and myself have had, as I perceive, no effect upon Crito.[1]

Notice here what seems to be Socrates' major presupposition. He distinguishes between himself and his body which is soon to be lifeless; and he says that he will continue to live even when his body is lifeless. Evidently, then, Socrates thinks of his real self as something distinct from his body.

And in thinking of life after death it is of the continued existence of this non-bodily self that he is thinking.

And that is how people think when they support the first of our views about life after death. For, according to this, people are not to be identified with their bodies and they will survive their deaths in non-bodily form. As I say, this view has a long history in philosophy. Apart from Plato, a particularly famous exponent of it is Descartes:

My essence consists solely in the fact that I am a thinking thing (or a substance whose whole essence or nature is to think). And although possibly (or rather certainly, as I shall say in a moment) I possess a body with which I am very intimately conjoined, yet because, on the one side, I have a clear and distinct idea of myself inasmuch as I am only a thinking and unextended thing, and as, on the other, I possess a distinct idea of body, inasmuch as it is only an extended and unthinking thing, it is certain that this I (that is to say, my soul by which I am what I am), is entirely and absolutely distinct from my body, and can exist without it.[2]

Nor, we might add, is the view that persons are really distinct from their bodies one confined to philosophical circles. Poets, for example, have often traded on it, as, for instance, John Donne does in *The Ecstasy*:

> But O alas, so long, so far
> Our bodies why do we forbear?
> They are ours, though they are not we, we are
> The intelligences, they the sphere.

So much, then, for the first view on life after death. The second is very different. As we have seen, the first view depends on the premise that human beings are essentially distinct from their bodies and that life after death can be thought of in non-bodily terms. But the second view holds that the notion of life after death is in fact the notion of a bodily life. When we die our bodies corrupt and decay, or they are destroyed. So much seems incontestable. But according to the second view we shall, after death, continue to live on in some kind of bodily way. In fact, so the suggestion goes, we shall rise again. Thus we come to the notion of resurrection, a notion which for some people is an essential part of any credible belief in life after death. Thus Peter Geach writes: 'Apart from the *possibility* of resurrection, it seems to me a mere illusion to have any hope for life after death. I am of the mind of Judas Maccabeus: if there is no resurrection, it is superfluous and vain to pray for the dead.'[3] This position can be linked with that of Aquinas. He agrees that it is possible to talk in some sense about disembodied survival after death. He holds, for example, that one can coherently suppose the existence of souls separated from their bodies but capable of knowledge and understanding. But he is quite clear that full or perfect human existence depends on the union of soul and body so that, in Aquinas's view, when a human being, P, dies, it must be said that something has really ceased to be and that P will not properly live as a full and perfect human being until his body is raised from the dead. 'Elements that are by nature destined for union', he says,

naturally desire to be united with each other; for any being seeks what is suited to it by nature. Since, therefore, the natural condition of the human soul is to be united to the body . . . it has a natural desire for union with the body. Hence the will cannot be perfectly at rest until the soul is again joined to the body. When this takes place, man rises from the dead. . . . By nature the soul is a part of man as his form. But no part is perfect in its nature unless it exists in its whole. Therefore man's final happiness requires the soul to be again united to the body.[4]

Here, then, are two distinct views of life after death. According to the first we shall survive as disembodied selves. According to the second we shall rise again in bodily form. But what are we to make of such views? Philosophers have raised two questions. The first can be regarded as conceptual. It basically asks whether or not our two views of life after death are possible, whether *could* be what our two views say there *will* be. The second question, however, moves from possibility to actuality. It asks whether it is reasonable to believe that we can look forward to disembodied survival or resurrection. Let us therefore consider each question in turn. And to begin with let us start by asking what kind of answer can be given when it is directed to the notion of non-bodily survival.

The survival of the disembodied self

If human beings are not to be identified with their bodies then, as Descartes says, there seems no obvious reason why they cannot exist without their bodies. And if human beings can exist without their bodies then the view that they can survive death seems a plausible one. We normally think of death as the end of a person's bodily life. But if a person is distinct from his body then the fact that his body dies does not entail that he dies.

But is it correct to think of human beings as distinct from their bodies in such a way that it is possible for them to exist in a disembodied state? Descartes, as we have seen, thought that it is; and he certainly does not lack supporters. A particularly trenchant supporter of Descartes is H. D. Lewis. 'My own conclusion', says Lewis, 'is that no recent discussions of the mind–body problem have succeeded in showing that we can dispense with an absolute distinction between mind and body.'[5] 'I have little doubt', he declares, 'that there are mental processes quite distinct from observable behaviour and that each individual has an access to his own experiences in having them which is not possible for the most favoured observer.'[6]

The theory of Descartes and Lewis, that persons are essentially other than their bodies, is usually referred to as Dualism. And dualism, I think we can say, is an enormously attractive and powerful theory. A number of points seem, at first glance, to tell in its favour. For one thing there is the fact that we often naturally talk as if our real selves were distinct from our bodies – as, for instance, when we say that we *have* our bodies, and as when we agree that we can be the same persons over a number of years even though our bodily make-up has drastically changed in the meantime. Another factor to be reckoned with is the way that we seem to have a privileged access to many of our thoughts and feelings. We can think about something and we can have emotions towards things without displaying the fact by any bodily behaviour. Even if someone were to look at our brains as we were thinking about things they would not see our thoughts. All of this is admirably brought out by Lewis. As he says, we may identify Brown by pointing to a man lighting his pipe; but

We are also apt to think that there is more than the physical movement, the motions of the hands are intended and there is much else that goes on in Brown's life at this moment. He may have a far-away look and although he seems to get his pipe to draw we may also say that he is not 'with us', he is thinking of the fish he will catch in the lake this afternoon. At these times we are apt to draw a sharp distinction between mind and body, Brown is physically here but his mind is 'far away', and while we no longer take 'far away' in a literal sense we come vividly to think that there is a good deal more involved in being Brown than the movements and location of his body. There is also something 'going on in his mind' as well. . . . The dichotomy of mind and body comes easily to us in many contexts, whether or not it is ultimately warranted. . . . In some contexts at least, it is natural to think of ourselves as composite entities, as being (or having) a mind and a body. A person can have a deformed body and an excellent mind. . . . In what other way, it might be argued, could we think of ourselves except as some kind of composite beings having a mind as well as a body?[7]

Another fact that might be advanced in favour of a dualistic view of human beings is the way in which it might be totally reasonable to accept a dualistic view should we be confronted with certain conceivable circumstances. Might we not, for example, just have to accept that, given certain conceivable states of affairs, some person can continue to exist even though what we take to be his body has perished?

Some writers have argued that the right answer to this question is clearly negative. Take, for example, Bernard Williams.[8] He holds that in order for P to continue in existence P's body must continue in existence. Thus Williams holds that bodily continuity is a necessary condition of personal identity, and, in arguing his case, he asks us to consider the following situation. Suppose Charles claims to be Guy Fawkes, and suppose that he provides evidence of knowing things that Guy Fawkes would be likely to know. A dualist might be prepared to say that Charles is actually Guy Fawkes and that bodily continuity is not a necessary condition of personal identity. But, says Williams, if one person can claim to be Guy Fawkes, and if one person can provide evidence of knowing things that Guy Fawkes would be likely to have known, it is possible for two people simultaneously to claim to be Guy Fawkes and it is possible for two people simultaneously to provide evidence of knowing things that Guy Fawkes would be likely to have known. 'What', asks Williams, 'should we say in that case?'[9] He continues:

They cannot both be Guy Fawkes; if they were, Guy Fawkes would be in two places at once, which is absurd. . . . Hence we could not say that they were both identical with Guy Fawkes. We might instead say that one of them was identical with Guy Fawkes, and that the other was just like him; but this would be an utterly vacuous manoeuvre, since there would be *ex hypothesi* no principle determining which description was to apply to which. So it would be best, if anything, to say that both had mysteriously become like Guy Fawkes, clairvoyantly knew about him, or something like this. If this would be the best description of each of the two, why would it not be the best description of Charles if Charles alone were changed?[10]

But in reply to Williams it can surely be said that we may not be confronted by two people who give evidence of being one and the same person. We may be confronted only by one person claiming to be somebody in particular. And what should we say then? Suppose, for example, an intimate friend of mine, a lover shall we say, suddenly disappears without trace. Suppose further that somebody who looks totally unlike this person turns up and claims to be my long-lost lover. The time may surely come when I am rationally obliged, puzzled about things though I may be, to conclude that the claim is correct. I may, of course, be wrong; but that proves nothing. Nor does the fact that I may certainly have no idea of how my lover has come to be present to me with an appearance totally unlike that which I expect.

So it does not seem as if the dualistic view of persons is wholly implausible. Having said this, however, I think it now needs to be added that there are some fairly formidable objections to saying that we can therefore conclude that human beings can survive their deaths in a disembodied state. For even if we allow that people are more than we can observe, and even if we allow that circumstances may make it reasonable to conclude that some unfamiliar-looking body actually belongs to some intimate friend, there are difficulties in concluding that one can exist as a human person without a body.

For the fact is that much of our understanding of 'person' involves reference to the existence and processes of bodies. Dualists have replied to this point by insisting that persons can have a very vigorous and lively 'inner' life; that they can, for example, think and have emotional experiences without showing so by any kind of overt bodily behaviour. And this is certainly true, which is why it is easy to sympathize with much of the criticism levelled by philosophers of the twentieth century against a famous attack on dualism launched by Gilbert Ryle (1900–76) in his celebrated and influential book *The Concept of Mind*.[11] Ryle sometimes spoke as if people's history is simply detectable from their bodily behaviour, which seems false, if only because one can keep certain thoughts and feeling entirely to oneself. But to be alive as a human person is also to be able to engage in all sorts of activities which would be impossible in the absence of a body. Take, for example, thinking. We think about what we are doing, we act thoughtfully, and a proper account of thinking, therefore, seems to require a reference to behaviour and to physical context. The same applies to seeing. A full account of seeing will have to take notice of such sentences as 'I can't see, it's too dark', 'Let's see if he's finished', 'I saw my friend yesterday'. In this connection we can note some pertinent remarks of Peter Geach:

Well, how do we eventually use such words as 'see', 'hear', 'feel', when we have got into the way of using them? We do not exercise these concepts only so as to pick out cases of seeing and the rest in our separate world of sense-experience; on the contrary, these concepts are used in association with a host of other concepts relating, e.g., to the physical characteristics of what is seen and the behaviour of those who do see. In saying this I am not putting forward a theory, but just reminding you of very familiar features in the everyday use of the verb 'to see' and related expressions; our ordinary talk about seeing would cease to be intelligible if there were cut out of it such expressions as 'I can't see, it's too far off ', 'I caught his eye', 'Don't look round', etc. . . . I am not asking you to believe that 'to see' is itself a word for a kind of behaviour. But the concept of seeing can be maintained only because it has threads of connexion with these other non-psychological concepts; break enough threads and the concept of seeing collapses.[12]

Some writers have insisted on the importance of the existence of bodies as far as the existence of persons is concerned, and they have concluded that persons are nothing but bodies. I refer here to what has been called Behaviourism, and also to the so-called Identity-Thesis, according to some versions of which thought, feelings, and so forth are identical with brain processes.[13] But to point to the importance of the body in our understanding of persons is not necessarily to subscribe to forms of behaviourism or the identity-thesis. It is just to say that it is extremely difficult to defend a view which allows persons to be essentially distinct from their bodies, a view which allows that there can be bodiless persons recognizable as human beings.

To put it all another way, while we can easily agree that much of a person's life is private, and while we can even agree that it is possible to conceive of certain intellectual experiences occurring in a way that does not seem to depend on physical location, if we are talking about the survival of human beings we are talking about the survival of complex entities that owe so much to being bodily that it seems impossible to say that, in the absence of a body, there can really be a human person. If, then, it is said that a human person can live on as a disembodied self, the appropriate response would seem to be a puzzled scepticism. Confronted by an unfamiliar body I may reasonably conclude that I am dealing with my long-lost lover. But if I am told that my lover is a disembodied person I may reasonably take leave to say that whatever it is that is disembodied can hardly be human. There may be something there, but it could only be a shadow of what we mean by a human person.

Survival as resurrection

So there are strong conceptual objections to the claim that life after death is possible if thought of as the survival of people in a disembodied form. But what of the view that people can survive death by being raised in bodily form?

If it is possibility that we are concerned with, there is surely a case for holding that life after death is a possible notion if thought of in terms of resurrection. One reason for saying so should already be fairly clear. If the argument of the preceding section is correct, it would seem that anything that could be recognized as a human existence depends on the human person being a bodily individual. Now if one says that there is bodily life after death, one is at least talking about something that might, if it came about, be regarded as the life of a human person.

A second reason for saying that resurrection is possible lies in the fact that, given certain circumstances, one may have to conclude that somebody once dead has been raised to bodily life again. This is quite well brought out by John Hick who asks us to imagine certain extraordinary, but not logically impossible, states of affairs.

We begin with the idea of someone suddenly ceasing to exist at a certain place in this world and the next instant coming into existence at another place which is not contiguous with the first. He has not moved from A to B by making a path through the intervening space but has disappeared at A and reappeared at B. For example, at some learned gathering in London one of the company suddenly and inexplicably disappears and the next moment an exact 'replica' of him suddenly and inexplicably appears at some comparable meeting in New York. The person who appears in New York is exactly similar, as to both bodily and mental characteristics, to the person who disappears in London. There is continuity of memory, complete similarity of bodily features, including fingerprints, hair and eye coloration and stomach con-

tents, and also of beliefs, habits and mental propensities. In fact there is everything
that would lead us to identify the one who appeared with the one who disappeared,
except continuous occupancy of space.[14]

Now, as Hick says, this is a logically possible sequence of events. And
the reasonable verdict on the whole sequence may just have to be that the
person who appears in New York is the same as the one who disappeared
in London. For, as Hick says, the person in America may act and behave
just as we expect the person in London to. He may be as baffled by
appearing in New York as anybody else. All his friends and relations may
stoutly declare that he is quite definitely the person who went to the
meeting in London.

But suppose now that the sequence of events is slightly different. 'Let
us suppose that the event in London is not a sudden and inexplicable
disappearance, and indeed not a disappearance at all, but a sudden death.
Only, at the moment when the individual dies a "replica" of him as he was
at the moment before his death, and complete with memory up to that
instant, comes into existence in New York.'[15]

Faced with the first sequence of events it could be reasonable, as Hick
says, to extend our concept of 'the same person' to cover this strange new
case. Faced with this second sequence might one not be justified in doing
so again? As Hick argues, one might be.

Even with the corpse on our hands it would still, I suggest, be an extension of 'same
person' required and warranted by the postulated facts to say that the one who died
has been miraculously re-created in New York. The case would, to be sure, be even
odder than the previous one because of the existence of the dead body in London
contemporaneously with the living person in New York. And yet, striking though
the oddness undoubtedly is, it does not amount to a logical impossibility. Once
again we must imagine some of the deceased's colleagues going to New York to
interview the person who has suddenly appeared there. He would perfectly remember them and their meeting, be interested in what had happened, and be as amazed
and dumbfounded about it as anyone else; and he would perhaps be worried about
the possible legal complications if he should return to London to claim his property
and so on. Once again, I believe, they would soon find themselves thinking of him
and treating him as the same person as the dead Londoner. Once again the factors
inclining us to say that the one who died and the one who appeared are the same
person would far outweigh the factors inclining us to say that they are different
people. Once again we should have to extend our usage of 'same person' to cover
the new case.[16]

In short, logically conceivable circumstances could justify us in concluding that someone known to have died has returned to life in a bodily
form. And if belief in resurrection is belief that such circumstances could
come to pass, then the belief is a possible one. That is to say, resurrection
is logically possible.

Reasons for belief in life after death

I shall be returning at the end of this chapter to some further conceivability questions about life after death. But for the moment we can now move on to the question of whether it is reasonable to hold that on either of the above views of life after death there is such a thing.

One reason that has been offered for saying that it is can be dealt with very briefly. This is not because the reason is trivial or silly or not worth investigating at length; it is just that it cannot be properly assessed in this book. It takes the form of an experimental argument for life after death and is entirely based on psychical research. Such research examines claims to the effect that persons known to be dead have actually communicated with living people by means of mediums. A great deal of effort has been directed to this research and many have considered that its results make it reasonable to believe in life after death.

But the simple fact remains that psychical research presents a vast amount of data on which there is considerable disagreement among those who have studied it. In talking about the question of miracle I suggested in Chapter 11 that any final verdict would have to depend on detailed examination of particular cases. It seems reasonable to say that the same applies to any argument for life after death based on psychical research. And since this book is not an examination of such research, it also seems that this is not the place to pronounce on what can be gleaned from it. We can, however, note that there are philosophers who have thought that it may prove significant. Thus, for example, Hick suggests that 'even if we discount the entire range of psychical phenomena, it remains true that the best cases of trance utterance are impressive and puzzling, and taken at face value are indicative of survival and communication after death.' He continues: 'If, through a medium, one talks with an intelligence that gives a coherent impression of being an intimately known friend who has died and who established identity by a wealth of private information and indefinable personal characteristics – as has occasionally happened – then we cannot dismiss without careful trial the theory that what is taking place is the return of a consciousness from the spirit world.'[17]

But if it is not possible for us to engage with the experimental argument for life after death, it is still possible to say something about the philosophical arguments that have been advanced. They take various forms, but two of the most popular argue from the nature of the self and from morality.

The first form of argument runs roughly as follows. How is it that things pass out of existence? The answer is by means of a dissolution of parts which usually comes about because of the action of some exterior force. Thus a man's body can perish because something harms it, thereby causing it to break up in some sense. The human person, on the other hand, is not to be identified with a body. The human self is really a non-material and unextended entity. But if this is the case, then it cannot pass out of existence by means of a dissolution of parts. And since it is not a material thing, it is hard to see how something can exert any force on it so as to bring about its destruction. The human person is therefore immortal.

But this argument is surely a very weak one. For one thing it evidently presupposes that a person could be said to live as a disembodied self, and we have already seen reason for questioning that view. But even allowing that the view is correct, there are difficulties with the argument. Perhaps things generally do seem to pass out of existence because some kind of physical deterioration takes place in them, and perhaps we can speak here about a dissolution of parts. Perhaps too we can normally explain the destruction of things by referring to something that is acting upon them in some way. But none of this entitles us to claim any certainty that things can only cease to exist because they have parts that can dissolve. Nor can we claim that something can only cease to exist because something physical has acted on it. For it is surely possible that there should be things that just cease to exist and that human beings are such things. At any rate, unless one holds that human beings continue to exist of logical necessity, which does not seem a very plausible supposition, it seems hard to see how this possibility can be ruled out.

A famous version of the moral argument for life after death can be found in Kant. Earlier on we saw that Kant holds that it is possible to move from the fact of moral obligation to the existence of God. But he also holds that moral obligation has implications for life after death:

The realization of the *summum bonum* in the world is the necessary object of a will determinable by the moral law. But in this will the *perfect accordance* of the mind with the moral law is the supreme condition of the *summum bonum*. This then must be possible, as well as its object, since it is contained in the command to promote the latter. Now the perfect accordance of the will with the moral law is *holiness*, a perfection of which no rational being of the sensible world is capable at any moment of his existence. Since, nevertheless, it is required as practically necessary, it can only be found in a progress *in infinitum* towards that perfect accordance, and on the principles of pure practical reason it is necessary to assume such a practical progress as the real object of the will. Now, this endless progress is only possible on the supposition of an *endless* duration of the *existence* and personality of the same rational being (which is called the immortality of the soul). The *summum bonum*, then, practically is only possible on the supposition of the immortality of the soul; consequently this immortality, being inseparably connected with the moral law, is a postulate of pure practical reason (by which I mean a *theoretical* proposition, not demonstrable as such, but which is an inseparable result of an unconditional *a priori* practical law).[18]

But this argument too does not provide very good reason for believing in life after death. Some people, of course, would dismiss it at once because, as we have seen, they would reject any notion of a moral law over and against them. They would, for example, say that moral judgements are grounded on something like subjective feeling. But even if such people are wrong, it is implausible to argue that there are moral obligations that cannot be cancelled by death. Someone may say that he ought to do certain things, and he may regret that he cannot do them this side of the grave. But if he really cannot do them, then it is wrong to say that he ought to do them. Kant, of course, will reply that a person can actually do what he ought even though he cannot do so in this life. For, according to Kant, the existence of God is a guarantee that the *summum bonum* will finally be realized. But, as I argued in Chapter 10, Kant's argument for God as ensuring the realization of the *summum bonum* is itself a weak one. If one could rely on there being a God to provide a context where the *summum bonum* can be realized, then it might be reasonable to hold that human beings will survive their deaths as part of the grand realization. But Kant's case for saying that there is such a God is not convincing.

Can it be restated so as to seem so? Some would argue that it can. It has been urged that morality is really pointless if there is no life after death. For this reason, it is sometimes said, the basic thrust of Kant's argument is correct. Others have maintained that if God exists he can be expected to give people life after death, for he is powerful and benevolent and would surely not leave us with nothing but the prospect of extinction. This argument is often supplemented by appeal to God's justice. God, it is said, is just and justice requires that evil men should be punished and good ones rewarded. Therefore God will punish evil men and reward good ones and, since he cannot do so until they have reached the end of their lives, he will do so when they die, in which case there is life after death.

But these arguments are also very weak. Why say that morality is pointless if there is no life after death? If there is any point in being moral in this life, then morality *ipso facto* has a point without reference to life after death. And for many people, of course, morality makes perfectly good sense in thoroughly worldly terms — think back to the position of Geach touched on in Chapter 10. As for the view that the existence of God guarantees the inevitability of life after death, that too is open to question. Let us suppose that God exists. Can we then be sure that he will bring it about that people survive death? A lot here depends on one's view of God. If one thinks of God as a just moral agent, and if one thinks of God as having the power to make people survive their deaths, one might plausibly conclude that he will ensure that people survive death. For that is what a just moral agent with the necessary power is likely to do. But, as I argued in Chapter 3, we do not have to think of God as a moral agent at all. And if this view is accepted, then nothing can be inferred about the likelihood of his behaving as such. If God is not a moral agent, one cannot argue about him on the contrary assumption; that would be like predicting the behaviour of dogs on the basis of our knowledge of elephants.

Must we, then, conclude that it is not reasonable to believe in life after death? No, for there may be excellent arguments for life after death that I have not considered. But we have now examined some classical philosophical arguments for life after death, and these are not convincing. So perhaps we can here conclude on an agnostic note. Life after death is possible, but we have seen no decisive philosophical reason for believing in it. Many religious believers would say that there are other reasons for belief in life after death. According to them, we can be sure that people survive death because survival after death is an item of faith. But this view involves theological considerations that cannot be properly entered into here. In assessing it, we would obviously have to consider the whole question of religious faith. This, in turn, would lead us to other questions, particularly ones about revelation and religious dogma.

The desirability of life after death

I have so far suggested that life after death is possible. I have also suggested that certain arguments in favour of it are open to question. In conclusion, I would now like to say something about a problem concerning belief in life after death which is rarely considered, but which evidently interests some people. Suppose it could be shown that there is reason to believe in life after death. Would that mean that human beings have anything to look forward to?

This may seem a strange question. Is life not intrinsically desirable? Who in his right mind would choose to pass out of existence? Is not the prospect of extinction a terrible one? But even if we accept that it is possible for someone to survive physical death, there still remain difficulties about the attractiveness of life after death. One of them springs from the ways in which people currently live. Some people are beautiful, healthy, happy, and intelligent. But some are ugly, sick, suffering, and stupid. Does this not mean that survival after death is not necessarily a good thing? And does it not also mean that there is something fundamentally wrong about belief in life after death?

Some have held that any kind of life is better than extinction. A good example is Miguel de Unamuno (1864–1936). 'For myself,' he writes, 'I can say that as a youth, and even as a child, I remained unmoved when shown the most moving pictures of hell, for even then nothing appeared to me quite so horrible as nothingness itself.'[19] Elsewhere he declares: 'I do not want to die – no; I neither want to die nor do I want to want to die;

I want to live for ever and ever and ever. I want this "I" to live – this poor "I" that I am and that I feel myself to be here and now, and therefore the problem of the duration of my soul, of my own soul, tortures me.'[20] But people who believe in life after death have rarely spoken about it as nothing but the alternative to extinction. They have presented it as something to look forward to, as something desirable. And for this reason our present question about it remains. Is life after death worth having?

It seems to me extremely difficult to show the desirability of life after death on one view of survival. This is the view that a person can survive death in non-bodily form. Even if we accept it, even if we waive the objections to it raised earlier, the life it holds out for us is surely bleak indeed.

This point is well made by Bernard Williams in dialogue with H. D. Lewis. According to Lewis, we can believe in a non-bodily life after death if we think of it either as involving experiences like those we have when dreaming, or as a state of living in 'a world of thoughts alone'.

If my body were whisked away while I dream and I nonetheless continued to have a coherent dream experience, this could be an excellent model of one sort of after life we may envisage. . . . The same principles apply in essentials, but obviously in ways we find harder to anticipate, if we think of the remaining alternative. . . . We may approach it if we think of ourselves so deeply absorbed in some intellectual activity that we become almost oblivious of our bodies and our surroundings and suppose that our bodies were then whisked away and we continued with our train of thought.[21]

Williams replies to all this by referring to Lewis's first alternative. This, he says,

makes the whole of future life into a kind of delusion. It is very like perceiving . . . but it obviously is not perceiving, in just the same way that dreaming is not perceiving and it seems to me that one thing I do not want to do is to spend the rest of eternity in a delusive simulacrum of perceptual activity. That just seems to me a rather lowering prospect. Why should a future of error be of interest to me?

Talking of Lewis's 'world of thoughts alone', Williams continues:

The alternative was the slightly higher-minded alternative, that it might consist of purely intellectual activity, which of course many philosophers have seen as the ideal future. I can see why *they* might be particularly interested in it; others might be less so. . . . I mean, suppose that the prospects of Heaven or the future life are those of intellectual contemplation and I am a jolly, good hearted fun-loving sensual character from the seaside, these prospects appear to me to command very little hold on one's loyalty.[22]

So if life after death is something to look forward to, it would have to involve more than is possible on the picture of it provided by a theory of a disembodied future. But it would also have to involve more than bodily resurrection, if that is understood as nothing but the continuation of our present mode of life. For, as I said above, some people's lives are not all that desirable.

But this does not mean that they cannot become so. Suppose we continue with the notion of life after death as conceived in terms of resurrection. That would mean continuing with the model of life after death as a continued physical life for the people who have died. Now many people suffer from various disadvantages in this life. But it is surely possible that these disadvantages could be removed without the people who suffer from them ceasing to be human beings. For as long as we are dealing with a human being we are dealing with something that could, logically speaking, be relieved of its disadvantages without ceasing to be a human being. Take, for example, an extreme disadvantage such as that which might follow from severe brain damage. Let us suppose that someone suffers such damage but continues to live. We may say that his life is not worth living, that he has become a human vegetable, but we would hesitate, I think, to say that he had ceased to be a human being. Certainly he would be very different. But he would not be a different kind of thing; becoming a human vegetable is not the same as becoming a real vegetable. And if a human vegetable were somehow relieved of his disadvantages, then it would make sense to say that a human being had been restored to full human life.

In this way, I think, it is possible to suggest that life after death, conceived of in terms of resurrection, could be attractive. For while it is not desirable for human beings to continue to exist after death in just the way that many of them do now, it would surely be desirable for them to continue to exist after death without the various currently prevailing impediments to an enjoyable life. And the desirability of their doing so would be increased if there were reason to believe that, after death, human beings have available to them sources of enjoyment or happiness that are presently unknown. If, then, the notion of resurrection is not a conceptually impossible one, resurrection could well be an attractive prospect.

And there, perhaps, we can leave things, for the development of such reflection would involve more space than is available here. If the reader wishes to follow up things for himself, he will find relevant material mentioned in the bibliography. But just to round off the present chapter we can, on the basis of what has been argued, suggest that an attractive form of life after death is not to be dismissed as impossible, though we have seen no compelling reason to believe in life after death in any form. Many religious writers say a good deal more than this, but their suggestions raise a whole host of topics the pursuit of which would take me further afield than I can now travel.

Notes

Chapter 1. *Verification and falsification*

1. David Hume, *An Enquiry concerning Human Understanding*, ed. L.A. Selby-Bigge (3rd edn., Oxford, 1975), p.165.
2. 'Logische Analyse des Wahrscheinlichkeitsbegriffs', *Erkenntnis* (1930-1), **1**.
3. Rudolf Carnap, 'The Elimination of Metaphysics Through Logical Analysis of Language' in A. J. Ayer (ed.), *Logical Positivism* (Glencoe, Illinois, 1959), p.63.
4. Ayer (ed.), p.63
5. A. J. Ayer, *Language, Truth and Logic* (1st edn., 1936; 2nd edn., London, 1946.) References here are to the 2nd edn.
6. Ayer, *Language, Truth and Logic*, p.115.
7. Reprinted in Basil Mitchell (ed.), *The Philosophy of Religion* (London, 1971).
8. Mitchell (ed.), p.13.
9. ibid. p.21.
10. Moritz Schlick, 'Meaning and Verification', reprinted in Herbert Feigl and Wilfrid Sellars (ed.), *Readings in Philosophical Analysis* (New York, 1949).
11. Richard Swinburne, *The Coherence of Theism* (Oxford, 1977), p.27.
12. ibid. p.28.
13. Ayer, *Language, Truth and Logic*, pp.38 f.
14. ibid. p.13.
15. ibid.
16. London, 1973.
17. Review of *Language, Truth and Logic* (2nd edn.) in *Journal of Symbolic Logic* (1949), pp.52 f.

Chapter 2. *Talking about God*

1. Moses Maimonides, *The Guide for the Perplexed*, trans. M. Friedlander (London, 1936), pp.86 ff.
2. *Summa Theologiae* (S.T.), 1a, 13, 5 (Blackfriars edn., vol. 3, trans. Herbert McCabe, O.P., London and New York, 1964).
3. ibid.
4. ibid.
5. ibid.
6. ibid.
7. Ludwig Wittgenstein, *Philosophical Investigations*, trans. G. E. M. Anscombe (Oxford, 1968), para. 66.

8. 'Analogy Today', *Philosophy* (1976), **51,** 445.
9. Peter Geach, *Reason and Argument* (Oxford, 1976), p.39.

Chapter 3. *God and evil*

1. H. P. Owen, *Concepts of Deity* (London, 1971), p.1.
2. Cf. Augustine, *Confessions,* book 7, chap. 5.
3. S.T. 1a, 2, 3 (obj.1).
4. Richard Swinburne, *The Existence of God* (Oxford, 1979).
5. Swinburne, *The Existence of God*, pp.210 f.
6. ibid. pp.210 ff.
7. John Hick, *Evil and the God of Love* (2nd edn., London, 1977), pp.336 ff.
8. D. Z. Phillips, *The Concept of Prayer* (London, 1965), p.93.
9. ibid.
10. Dostoevsky, *The Brothers Karamazov,* trans. Constance Garnett (London, 1950), vol.1, part II, book V, chap. IV, p.250.
11. Cf. Ludwig Wittgenstein, 'A Lecture on Ethics', *The Philosophical Review* (1965), **74.**
12. Alvin Plantinga, *The Nature of Necessity* (Oxford, 1974), pp.166 f.
13. Owen, p.8.
14. Thomas Aquinas, *De Potentia*, III, 7. Author's translation.
15. S.T. 1a2ae, 79, 2 (Blackfriars edn., vol. 25, trans. John Fearon, London and New York, 1969).
16. Michael Durrant, *The Logical Status of 'God'* (London, 1973), p.46.
17. Owen, p.11.
18. Owen, p.23.

Chapter 4. *The ontological argument*

1. Anselm, *Proslogion,* trans. M. J. Charlesworth (Oxford, 1965), chap. II. It is most important to point out that scholarly interpretations of Anselm's whole programme in the *Proslogion* differ widely and that the interpretation presupposed here (which is probably the most common among philosophers of religion) is by no means indisputable and certainly calls for various qualifications which space here prohibits. For material on Anselm see the Bibliography.
2. In *The Philosophical Works of Descartes*, vol. I, trans. Elizabeth S. Haldane and G. R. T. Ross (Cambridge, 1911).
3. Descartes, op. cit. p.181.
4. Norman Malcolm, 'Anselm's Ontological Arguments', reprinted in John Hick (ed.), *The Existence of God* (London and New York, 1964), pp.48–70.
5. Malcolm, p.56.
6. Cf. Robert C. Stalnaker, 'Possible Worlds' in Ted Honderich and Myles Burnyeat (ed.), *Philosophy As It Is* (London, 1979).
7. Alvin Plantinga, *The Nature of Necessity*, p.213.
8. Plantinga, p.214.
9. See Charlesworth, op.cit., p.175.
10. Alvin Plantinga, *God, Freedom and Evil* (London, 1975), p.91.

11. Immanuel Kant, *Critique of Pure Reason*, trans. Norman Kemp Smith (London, 1964), pp.502 f.
12. *The Coherence of Theism*, p.264.
13. *Critique of Pure Reason*, pp.504 f.
14. *The Philosophical Works of Descartes*, vol. 2, trans. Elizabeth S. Haldane and G. R. T. Ross (Cambridge, 1912), p.186.
15. Cf. Peter Geach, 'Form and Existence' in *God and the Soul* (London, 1969).
16. Cf. D. P. Henry, *Medieval Logic and Metaphysics* (London, 1972), III, 7.
17. John Hick, 'A Critique of the "Second Argument"', in John Hick and Arthur McGill (ed.), *The Many Faced Argument* (London, 1968), pp.353 f.

Chapter 5. *The cosmological argument*

1. S.T. 1a, 2, 3 (Blackfriars edn., vol. 2, trans. Timothy McDermott, London and New York, 1964).
2. Cf. Anthony Kenny, *The Five Ways* (London, 1969), chap. 1.
3. Descartes's argument can be found in his *Meditations*.
4. Clarke's argument is given in his Boyle lectures of 1704, published as *A Demonstration of The Being and Attributes of God*.
5. G. W. Leibniz, *A Resumé of Metaphysics* in G. H. R. Parkinson (ed.), *Leibniz: Philosophical Writings* (London and Toronto, 1973), p.145.
6. *The Five Ways*, p.28.
7. ibid. p.21.
8. ibid. pp.22 f.
9. ibid. pp.43 f.
10. 'A Debate on the Existence of God', reprinted in John Hick (ed.), *The Existence of God*, pp.167-91.
11. John Hick, *Philosophy of Religion* (2nd edn., Englewood Cliffs, New Jersey, 1973), p.21.
12. Cf. Antony Flew, *An Introduction to Western Philosophy* (London, 1971), p.196.
13. *The Existence of God*, p.175.
14. Cf. Peter Geach, review of Kenny's *The Five Ways* in *Philosophical Quarterly* (1970), **20**, 311–12.
15. S.T. 1a, 3, 1.
16. David Hume, *An Enquiry concerning Human Understanding*, ed. L. A. Selby-Bigge (3rd edn., Oxford, 1975), p.63.
17. *The Letters of David Hume*, ed. J. Y. T. Greig (Oxford, 1932), vol. 1, p.187.
18. C. D. Broad, 'Kant's Mathematical Antinomies', *Proceedings of the Aristotelian Society*, **LV**, 10.
19. David Hume, *A Treatise of Human Nature*, ed. L. A. Selby-Bigge (Oxford, 1965), pp.79 f.
20. G. E. M. Anscombe, ' "Whatever Has a Beginning of Existence Must Have a Cause": Hume's Argument Exposed', *Analysis* (1974), **34**, 150.
21. *Enquiry*, p.136.
22. Cf. Michael Durrant, *Theology and Intelligibility* (London, 1973), pp.153 ff.

Chapter 6. *The argument from design*

1. Cicero, *The Nature of the Gods,* trans. Horace C. P. McGregor (Harmondsworth, 1972), p.124.
2. Richard Swinburne, 'The Argument from Design – A Defence', *Religious Studies* (1972), **8**, 193–205.
3. *Natural Theology* is Volume IV of *The Works of William Paley* (Oxford, 1838).
4. Paley, op.cit. p.1.
5. ibid. p.2.
6. ibid. p.13.
7. See *Critique of Pure Reason*, trans. Norman Kemp Smith (London, 1964).
8. Thomas McPherson, *The Argument from Design* (London, 1972), p.20.
9. *Enquiry*, p.136.
10. Norman Kemp Smith (ed.), *Hume's Dialogues concerning Natural Religion* (London, 1947), p.149.
11. *Dialogues*, pp.149 f.
12. See Richard Swinburne, 'The Argument from Design', *Philosophy* (1968), **43**, p.208.
13. *Dialogues*, p.160.
14. ibid. p.161.
15. ibid. pp.161 ff.
16. ibid. p.164.
17. ibid. p.163.
18. ibid. p.168.
19. Richard Swinburne, 'The Argument from Design', *Philosophy* (1968), **43**, p.205.
20. 'The Argument from Design', p.209.
21. *Dialogues*, p.167.
22. ibid. p.168.
23. Richard Swinburne, *The Existence of God*, pp.138 and 136.
24. 'The Argument from Design', p.211.
25. *The Existence of God*, pp.138 f.
26. Michael Dummett, 'Bringing About the Past' in *Truth And Other Enigmas* (London, 1978), pp.333–50.
27. *The Existence of God*, p.141.

Chapter 7. *Experience and God*

1. Ludwig Wittgenstein, *On Certainty*, ed. G. E. M. Anscombe and G. H. von Wright, trans. Denis Paul and G. E. M. Anscombe (Oxford, 1974), para. 164.
2. *On Certainty*, para. 166.
3. ibid. para. 167.
4. Ludwig Wittgenstein, *Philosophical Investigations*, paras. 485 and 217.
5. Cf. *The Complete Works of Saint Teresa of Jesus*, trans. E. Allison Peers (London 1946); Gerard Brennan, *St. John of the Cross* (Cambridge, 1973); Georges Morel, *Le Sens de l'Existence selon S. Jean de la Croix* (Paris, 1960-1, 2 vols.);

Walter Hilton, *The Scale of Perfection*, abridged and presented by Illtyd Trethowan (London, 1975).

6. H. D. Lewis, *Philosophy of Religion* (London, 1965), p.144.
7. H. D. Lewis, *Our Experience of God* (London, 1970), p.45.
8. *The Philosophy of Religion*, p.144.
9. *Philosophical Investigations*, pp.193 f.
10. 'Religious Faith as Experience-As', in *Talk of God*, ed. G. N. A. Vesey (London, 1969), pp.22 ff.
11. *Talk of God*, pp.23, 26, 27.

Chapter 8. *The attributes of God – 1 Eternity*

1. Boethius, *The Consolation of Philosophy*, book V, 6.
2. *Confessions*, book XI, 13.
3. *Proslogion*, chap. XIX.
4. pp.210 f.
5. Cf. Charles Hartshorne, *The Logic of Perfection* (La Salle, Illinois, 1962).
6. *The Coherence of Theism*, p.221.
7. *Aquinas: A Collection of Critical Essays* (London and Melbourne, 1969), p.263.
8. John L. McKenzie, *Dictionary of the Bible* (London, 1975), pp.247 f.
9. Grand Rapids, Michigan, 1965, p.202.
10. *The Coherence of Theism*, p.211.
11. ibid.

Chapter 9. *The attributes of God – 2 Omniscience*

1. 'Omniscience and Immutability', *Journal of Philosophy* (1966), **63,** 409-21.
2. A. N. Prior, 'The Formalities of Omniscience', *Philosophy* (1962), XXXVII, 116.
3. 'Omniscience and Indexical Reference', *Journal of Philosophy* (1967), **64,** 203–10.
4. S.T. 1a, 14, 13 (Blackfriars edn., vol. 4, trans. Thomas Gornall, London and New York, 1964).

Chapter 10. *Morality and religion*

1. Immanuel Kant, *Critique of Practical Reason*, trans. Thomas Kingsmill Abbott (London, New York and Toronto, 1909), pp.221 f.
2. H. P. Owen, *The Moral Argument for Christian Theism* (London, 1965), pp.49 f.
3. J. H. Newman, *A Grammar of Assent*, ed. C. F. Harrold (London and New York, 1947), p.83.
4. Cf. *Absolute Value* (London, 1970) and *Mysticism and Theology* (London, 1974).
5. *Absolute Value*, pp.84 f.
6. R. B. Braithwaite, *An Empiricist's View of the Nature of Religious Belief* (Cambridge, 1955), pp.19 and 32.
7. J. Rachels, 'God and Human Attitudes', *Religious Studies* (1971), **7**, p.334.
8. Such a line is advanced by Rousseau (1712–78) in *The Social Contract* (1762).
9. *De Rerum Natura*, I, 101.

10. Bertrand Russell, *Why I am not a Christian* (London, 1957), p.37.
11. Søren Kierkegaard, *Fear and Trembling*, trans. Robert Payne (London, New York and Toronto, 1939), pp.84 f.
12. D. Z. Phillips, 'God and Ought' in Ian Ramsey (ed.), *Christian Ethics and Contemporary Philosophy* (London, 1966), pp.137 f.
13. Cf. J. L. Mackie, *Ethics* (Harmondsworth, 1977).
14. Illtyd Trethowan, *The Basis of Belief* (London, 1960), p.117.
15. P. T. Geach, 'The Moral Law and the Law of God' in *God and the Soul* (London, 1969), p.121.
16. Cf. Braithwaite, pp.24 f.
17. Braithwaite, p.26.
18. London, 1968, p.61.
19. Philip L. Quinn, *Divine Commands and Moral Requirements* (Oxford, 1978), pp.6 f.
20. Ninian Smart, *The Phenomenon of Religion* (London and Oxford, 1978), p.10.
21. Paul Edwards (ed.), vol. 7 (New York and London, 1967).

Chapter 11. *Miracle*

1. *Enquiry*, p.115.
2. Thomas Aquinas, *Summa Contra Gentiles*, III, 2, chap. 101, trans. Vernon J. Bourke (New York, 1956), p.82.
3. ibid.
4. ibid. p. 83.
5. R. H. Fuller, *Interpreting the Miracles* (London, 1966), pp.8 f.
6. R. F. Holland, 'The Miraculous' in D. Z. Phillips (ed.), *Religion and Understanding* (Oxford, 1967), pp.155 f.
7. ibid. p. 157.
8. On the literary background to Hume's discussion of miracles see J. C. A. Gaskin, *Hume's Philosophy of Religion* (London, 1968), chap. 7.
9. *Enquiry*, p.125.
10. Antony Flew, *Hume's Philosophy of Belief* (London, 1961), p.186 f.
11. *Hume's Philosophy of Religion*, p.124.
12. *Enquiry*, p.127.
13. S.T. 1a, 105, 6 (Blackfriars edn., vol. 14, trans. T. C. O'Brien, London and New York, 1975).
14. ibid.
15. Richard Swinburne, *The Concept of Miracle* (London, 1970), p.57.
16. *Enquiry*, p.110.
17. ibid. pp.114 f.
18. ibid. pp.115 f.
19. ibid. p.116.
20. ibid. pp.116 f.
21. ibid. p.117.
22. ibid. pp.117 f.
23. ibid. p.118.
24. ibid.

25. ibid. p.119.
26. ibid. pp.121 f.
27. *Hume's Philosophy of Religion*, p.114.
28. *The Concept of Miracle*, p.60.

Chapter 12. *Life after death*

1. *The Dialogues of Plato*, trans. B. Jowett, vol. II (Oxford, 1871), p.263.
2. *Meditation* VI (*The Philosophical Works of Descartes*, trans. Elizabeth S. Haldane and G. R. T. Ross, vol. I, Cambridge, 1911, p.190).
3. *God and the Soul*, p.29.
4. Thomas Aquinas, *Compendium of Theology*, trans. Cyril Vollert (St. Louis and London, 1949), p.160.
5. *Philosophy of Religion*, p.286.
6. *Philosophy of Religion*, p.282. Cf. H. D. Lewis, *The Self and Immortality* (London, 1973), pp.62 and 68.
7. H. D. Lewis, *The Elusive Mind* (London, 1969), pp.16 f.
8. Bernard Williams, 'Personal Identity and Individuation', *Proceedings of the Aristotelian Society* (1956–7), **LVII**, 229–52.
9. Williams, p.238.
10. Williams, pp.238 f.
11. Gilbert Ryle, *The Concept of Mind* (London, 1949). For a good collection of essays on Ryle see Oscar P. Wood and George Pitcher (ed.), *Ryle* (London, 1971).
12. *God and the Soul*, p.29.
13. Cf. C. V. Borst (ed.), *The Mind/Brain Identity Thesis* (London, 1970).
14. John Hick, *Death and Eternal Life* (London, 1979), p.280.
15. *Death and Eternal Life*, p.284.
16. ibid.
17. *Philosophy of Religion*, p.105. Cf. H. D. Lewis, *Persons and Life after Death* (London, 1978), pp.38 ff.
18. *Critique of Practical Reason*, trans. Thomas Kingsmill Abbott (London, New York and Toronto, 1909), pp.218 f.
19. Miguel de Unamuno, *The Tragic Sense of Life* (London, 1962), p.28.
20. ibid. p.60.
21. *Persons and Life After Death*, pp.53 f.
22. ibid. pp.69 and 72.

Bibliography

Many of the works referred to in the notes to this book provide important reading matter for anyone interested in pursuing the philosophy of religion. This bibliography is mainly confined to useful material not so far mentioned.

Beginners in the philosophy of religion will benefit from some introductory works on philosophy and/or the history of philosophy. Particularly helpful are: A. J. Ayer, *The Central Questions of Philosophy* (London, 1973); F. C. Copleston, *History of Philosophy* (9 vols., London, 1946–74); John Hospers, *An Introduction to Philosophical Analysis* (2nd edn., London, 1967); D. J. O'Connor (ed.), *A Critical History of Western Philosophy* (London, 1964).

A good introduction to the writers commonly considered historically important for the philosophy of religion is M. J. Charlesworth, *Philosophy of Religion: The Historic Approaches* (London, 1972). Useful general introductions to the philosophy of religion are: John Hick, *Philosophy of Religion* (2nd edn., Englewood Cliffs, New Jersey, 1973); H. D. Lewis, *Philosophy of Religion* (London, 1965); Thomas McPherson, *The Philosophy of Religion* (London, 1965); William L. Rowe, *Philosophy of Religion* (Encino and Belmont, Ca.). Useful readers in the philosophy of religion are: James Churchill and David V. Jones, *An Introductory Reader in the Philosophy of Religion* (London, 1979); Basil Mitchell (ed.), *The Philosophy of Religion* (London, 1971); William L. Rowe and William J. Wainwright (ed.), *Philosophy of Religion: Selected Readings* (New York/Chicago/San Francisco/Atlanta, 1973).

For an introductory discussion of verificationism, falsificationism, and religious belief see Frederick Ferré, *Language, Logic and God* (London and Glasgow, 1970). For a more technical discussion see R. S. Heimbeck, *Theology and Meaning* (London, 1969). For an introduction to logical positivism see Oswald Hanfling (ed.), *Essential Readings in Logical Positivism* (Oxford, 1981). For useful material on analogy and related matters see: David B. Burrell, *Aquinas, God and Action* (London and Henley, 1979); E. L. Mascall, *Existence and Analogy* (London, 1966); Humphrey Palmer, *Analogy* (London, 1973); Patrick Sherry, *Religion, Truth and Language-Games* (London, 1977). A helpful textbook on philosophical problems about language is Bernard Harrison, *An Introduction to the Philosophy of Language* (London, 1979).

worth consulting are: M. B. Ahern, *The Problem of Evil* (London, 1971); A. Farrer, *Love Almighty and Ills Unlimited* (London, 1961).

For a good survey and discussion of the question of God's existence see Hans Küng, *Does God Exist?* (London, 1980). See also Robin Attfield, *God and the*

Secular (Cardiff, 1978); Hugo Meynell, *God and the World* (London, 1971).

As a background to the ontological argument in Anselm see: G. R. Evans, *Anselm and Talking About God* (Oxford, 1978); J. McIntyre, *St. Anselm and his Critics: A Reinterpretation of the Cur Deus Homo* (Edinburgh, 1954); R. W. Southern, *St. Anselm and his Biographer* (Cambridge, 1963). For a general discussion of the ontological argument see Jonathan Barnes, *The Ontological Argument* (London, 1972). An excellent reader on the ontological argument is John Hick and Arthur McGill (ed.), *The Many Faced Argument* (London, 1967).

A good survey of the history of the cosmological argument is William Lane Craig, *The Cosmological Argument from Plato to Leibniz* (London, 1980). A good discussion of the cosmological argument in Aquinas, Scotus (*c.*1266–1308), and Clarke is William Rowe, *The Cosmological Argument* (Princeton and London, 1975). Significant statements of the cosmological argument can be found in Plato, *Laws*, book X; Descartes, *Meditation* III; John Locke (1632–1704), *An Essay concerning Human Understanding*, book IV, chap. 10. For two modern attempts to advance a version of the cosmological argument see: Germain Grisez, *Beyond the New Theism* (Notre Dame and London, 1975); John J. Shepherd, *Experience, Inference and God* (London, 1975). For discussion of a rarely considered version of the cosmological argument (important in the history of Islamic thought) see William Lane Craig, *The Kalām Cosmological Argument* (London, 1979).

A good general work on the argument from design is Thomas McPherson, *The Argument from Design* (London, 1972). See also R. H. Hurlbutt, *Hume, Newton and the Design Argument* (Lincoln, 1965).

The claim to experience God is often discussed under the heading 'Religious Experience' or 'Mysticism'. Works that purport to deal with these topics may therefore be usefully considered with reference to experience of God. One might begin by looking at: Peter Donovan, *Interpreting Religious Experience* (London, 1979); S. Hook (ed.), *Religious Experience and Truth* (New York, 1961); H. J. N. Horsburgh, 'The Claims of Religious Experience', *Australasian Journal of Philosophy* (1957), **35**; Steven T. Katz (ed.), *Mysticism and Philosophical Analysis* (London, 1978); T. R. Miles, *Religious Experience* (London, 1972).

A useful study of eternity and timelessness is Nelson Pike, *God and Timelessness* (London, 1970). For an introduction to process theologians see John B. Cobb and David Ray Griffin, *Process Theology: An Introductory Exposition* (Belfast, 1976). For a Hartshorne bibliography see D. C. Hartshorne, 'Charles Hartshorne: Primary Bibliography', *Process Studies* (1976), VI, 1. Interesting theological discussions of divine eternity can be found in Karl Barth, *Church Dogmatics* II/1 (Edinburgh, 1957); Emile Brunner, *The Christian Doctrine of God* (*Dogmatics*, vol. 1, London, 1949); and Paul Tillich, *Systematic Theology*, vol. 1 (London, 1953). On divine omniscience see Peter Geach, *Providence and Evil* (Cambridge, 1977) and Robert Young, *Freedom, Responsibility and God* (London, 1975).

On issues relevant to the relationship between morality and religion, see: W. W. Bartley III, *Morality and Religion* (London, 1971); Peter Baelz, *Ethics and Belief* (London, 1977); Paul Helm (ed.), *Divine Commands and Morality* (Oxford, 1981); W. G. Maclagan, *The Theological Frontier of Ethics* (London, 1961); Kai Nielsen, *Ethics without God* (London and New York, 1973); Keith Ward, *Ethics and Chris-*

tianity (London, 1970). Students approaching the topic of morality and religion would benefit from some work on contemporary moral philosophy. Good introductions are: W. D. Hudson, *A Century of Moral Philosophy* (Guildford and London, 1980); D. D. Raphael, *Moral Philosophy* (Oxford, 1981); G. J. Warnock, *Contemporary Moral Philosophy* (London, 1967).

Useful essays relevant to Descartes on mind and body can be found in Willis Doney (ed.), *Descartes* (London and Melbourne, 1968). See also Bernard Williams, *Descartes: The Project of Pure Enquiry* (Harmondsworth, 1978). John Hick's *Death and Eternal Life* and H. D. Lewis's *The Self and Immortality* both contain extremely good bibliographies on matters relating to the topic of life after death.

Index